happiness
at work

Be Resilient, Motivated, and Successful—No Matter What

Srikumar S. Rao, Ph.D.

New York Chicago San Francisco Lisbon London Madrid Mexico City
Milan New Delhi San Juan Seoul Singapore Sydney Toronto

The *McGraw·Hill* Companies

Library of Congress Cataloging-in-Publication Data

Rao, Srikumar S.
    Happiness at work : be resilient, motivated, and successful—no matter what /
Srikumar S. Rao.
       p.   cm.
    Includes index.
    ISBN 13: 978-0-07-166432-5
    ISBN 10: 0-07-166432-7
    1. Job satisfaction.   2. Success in business.   3. Work—Psychological
aspects.   I. Title.

    HF5549.5.J63R34   2010
    650.1—dc22   2009052647

2 3 4 5 6 7 8 9 10 11 12 13 14 15 16   WFR/WFR   1 9 8 7 6 5 4 3 2 1 0

ISBN 978-0-07-166432-5
MHID   0-07-166432-7

Interior design by Monica Baziuk

McGraw-Hill books are available at special quantity discounts to use as premiums and
sales promotions or for use in corporate training programs. To contact a representative,
please e-mail us at bulksales@mcgraw-hill.com.

◉

To my wife, Meena,
without whose unstinting support I would never have
been able to write this or develop my course. There
were times—such as during my extended sojourns in
London—when she was almost a single mother, and
though the strain was great, the complaints were few.

◉

Contents

◘

Foreword

◙

I HAVE KNOWN SRIKUMAR Rao for many years and long admired his pioneering course "Creativity and Personal Mastery." Some of the professionals I most admire are alumni of this program, including the owner of one of the world's most prestigious restaurants, the CEO of an amazingly environmental-oriented nonprofit, a fantastic executive coach, and a spectacularly successful investment banker. They all agree that the concepts Dr. Rao shares have dramatically— and positively—changed their lives.

I believe that his great thoughts may be able to help you in the same way.

Happiness at Work: Be Resilient, Motivated, and Successful— No Matter What, its author, and its subject are especially significant to me because I attach great value to finding happiness and meaning in life. As a matter of fact, this is the subject of my new book, *Mojo*, in which I give my answer to the age-old question: What can people do to achieve more meaning and happiness in their lives? What a joy it is to know that Srikumar and I are on similar paths in our writing and our lives!

For much of my career as an executive coach, I have defined my mission as helping my clients achieve positive changes in their interpersonal behavior. Though this mission hasn't changed, I am now focusing more on our internal workings and on personal definitions of meaning and happiness. The stories, examples, suggestions, and teachings that Srikumar sets forth in *Happiness at Work* are highly supportive of this mission and have expanded my thinking on the subject altogether.

What I find most exciting about *Happiness at Work: Be Resilient, Motivated, and Successful—No Matter What* is the "no matter what" part of it. Srikumar delivers on this promise. In *Happiness at Work* he shows us how to find joy in the big—and little—things and how to do so anytime, anywhere. It will take a little practice and even a little work, but if you follow Srikumar's instructions you will enjoy the journey to having more happiness and meaning in your life, no matter what!

Life is good.

—Marshall Goldsmith

Million-selling author of
What Got You Here Won't Get You There;
Succession: Are You Ready?; and
*Mojo: How to Get It, How to Keep It, and
How to Get It Back If You Lose It*

Preface

◨

D O YOU SOMETIMES feel like a rag doll in the jaws of a hyperactive terrier—shaken vigorously from left to right, up and down, round and round, over and over again? Life can do that sometimes. But now it seems to be happening more often and the terrier has more muscular jaws and greater tenacity?

It's often said that the only constant is change, and stuff will come at you from left field. But what happens when the number of things from that field mysteriously increases and they all come at you with greater velocity and unerring accuracy?

The number of ways in which your life can be upended—despite all your careful planning—is almost comical. For example, an investment banker, conscious of the precariousness of his job, was determined not to buy more house than he could afford as so many of his peers were doing. He waited until his income was "secure," and he received a categorical assurance from his boss that he would be the very last person to be laid off in the event of a downturn. Then he bought his big house. Six months later, his 150-year-old bulge-bracket firm was whipsawed in the financial markets, ran out of capital, and folded, leaving him stranded high but not dry.

In another instance, a senior executive, who had a strong antipathy to one of her colleagues, was finally able to muster enough support to force him out. He joined another firm in a related industry. Less than a year later, that firm acquired hers in a hostile takeover. He became her new boss and promptly fired her.

Similar things may have happened to you, giving you strong empathy with a big-wave surfer caught by an unexpected tsunami and tumbled repeatedly. There are upheavals in career prospects, economic climate, and relationship dynamics. Frequently it becomes overwhelming.

You can survive. Even better, you can thrive. When the tsunami hits, you can surf it, and the speed and height are downright exhilarating. This book shows you how.

In my younger days, I sold big-budget marketing research projects to large companies. I floundered a lot until I started following the sage advice given to me by a grizzled veteran. He was a well-respected, experienced executive and looked on amusedly as I tried to engage him in small talk. I was trying to "establish rapport" and "build a connection." I was convinced that, in a world with many competent suppliers, relationships were the key to getting the sale.

After a few minutes, he cut in decisively, "Son, tell me what you have, why I should be interested, how much it costs, and why I should believe you." So I did.

Much later I asked him about his style and whether building affinity was important. "Of course it is," he replied. "But I'm busy and don't have time to chat with every salesperson trying to build a relationship with me. I don't even want one with most of them. I just want them to go away quickly. First, convince me that it's worth listening to you. Then deliver on your promise. Building rapport comes next and, in most cases, takes care of itself."

"How long do you give someone to make his case?" I asked.

"Thirty seconds," he replied. (I was just lucky. For some reason he'd given me five minutes.)

The same approach works for a book. I can sense you, the impatient reader, chafing at the bit. "Get on with it," you urge me silently. "Tell me what you have to offer, how I can benefit from it, and why I should trust you."

I understand and will comply. Here goes.

—————————— who you are ——————————

You are intelligent, ambitious, and on your way to success. But you're not quite sure exactly what success is. You do know that you are functioning far below your capacity, that you can accomplish much more than you presently are. Maybe you can honestly describe yourself as happy. But there is an undercurrent of dissatisfaction in your life, a sense that things could be better, that there is something you need to do. At times you wonder if the path you're taking through life is the right one for you.

Sometimes you feel as if you are walking on quicksand just fast enough that you are not sucked in completely. But you're going down all the same—slowly. You are unnerved by the turbulence that is everywhere—in financial markets, in international relations, in government activity, and in company maneuvers. Not overwhelmed, but somewhat queasy. You would like stability and something you can depend on. Your relationships are good, but they are not as deep and nourishing as you would like them to be. You have many friends, but there are few you would fight to keep and even fewer who you know with certainty will be in your life a few decades from now.

And, of course, you want to find purpose in your existence. You want to know that you matter, that your life is not in vain and your legacy is an honorable one.

If any two or more of the following statements are true of you, then this book will help you:

- ▣ You are working harder than ever but somehow seem to be accomplishing little.
- ▣ You have friends who you hardly ever see.
- ▣ You buy lots of stuff but notice the enjoyment is just not there.

▣ Your children grow up fast while you are away working to support them.

▣ Life seems to be passing you by while you strive to make a living.

▣ Items on your to-do list receive your best energy, and relationships get what's left.

▣ You confuse being busy with doing important stuff.

▣ You skip social events because you are "too busy."

▣ You have few close friends, and they are getting fewer.

▣ You can't relax; you grow restless if you have nothing to do.

▣ Wherever you are and whatever you're doing, you are conscious of time slipping away.

▣ You get bored easily. You *need* your iPod, music, TV, reading material, or some distraction.

▣ You cannot sit quietly by yourself for a half hour. (Try it before you answer this.)

▣ You sometimes miss meals and frequently overeat.

▣ You know there is more to life but are not clear what it is or how to get it.

what this book will teach you

This book will show you how to bring joy back into your life. It will return you to the halcyon days of your youth when you thought McDonald's was a four-star restaurant, when you preferred nickels to dimes because they were bigger, and when snow was an amazing experience and not a bother to be shoveled away.

That feeling of effervescence, that lightness of being, is what you will begin to taste again. You will cease being like Hamlet, "sicklied o'er with the pale cast of thought." When you smile, the sun will sulk and contemplate complaining to the authorities about unfair competition.

You won't get there immediately, but you will get there by and by if you do the exercises at the end of each chapter. And it won't be long before you experience a type of well-being that you forgot existed. Even Robert Browning's Pippa, contemplating the lark on the wing and the snail on the thorn, will envy you.

They say the world loves a happy bloke—or blokess, which I believe is the female equivalent—and you will indubitably become one. You will discover that funny, marvelous things happen as you find this wellspring of joy within yourself. Your relationships will improve. Your career will take off. Toxic people will leave your life.

That is what this book can do for you. I will give you the map and show you the road. But you have to make the journey.

why should you believe me?

Don't believe me. Why should you? I have a vested interest as the author of this book. But do skim through the chapters and see if what I say makes intuitive sense. If you find yourself nodding your head in agreement many times, then this book is for you.

Go back and actually do the exercises sincerely and conscientiously. See how your life is transformed.

—— how to get the most from this book ——

Since you bought this book (at least I hope you did!), you can certainly read it like a novel and put it aside. That is ineffective and not recommended. This book was written to help you make a profound transformation in your life, and such change does not happen quickly. The ideas presented are simple, and it's quite possible that you "know" many of the concepts already. But intellectual knowledge and agreement aren't much use. There is a huge difference between knowing that ice cream is cold and actually tasting it.

So by all means, skim the chapters if you want, but don't set it aside. Read a chapter every two or three days and really come to grips with it. Do the exercise at the end of each chapter and record your observations. Gather a group of like-minded friends and do the exercises together. Talk about your results and observations and discuss what worked, what didn't, and why.

You are embarking on a journey that will take unexpected turns, and there may be rough weather ahead. As with all journeys, it becomes more enjoyable if you have boon companions who can alert you to danger and save you if it strikes. And you, of course, will do the same for them.

So go forward with the thought that this is not a book to be read; it is to be experienced. Engage with it, wrestle with it, turn it upside down and peer into its crevices. If you expend significant emotional energy in this grappling, it will pay for itself tenfold or more in terms of the benefit you derive.

Hold on to the edge of your seat—here we go!

Acknowledgments

◙

I T IS NOT an easy task to gratefully acknowledge all those who contributed to making this book happen. Should I include everyone who helped shape me and made me what I am? That would require pages and pages of text and be tedious for you to read. Also, my publisher would object. Or should I simply include only those who directly helped with the writing and publishing? That would be a short list and would exclude many whose contributions were less obvious but still significant.

So I will compromise and simply name some individuals who helped a great deal with this book and the course on which it's based.

First, the people involved with the book:

◙ Lisa Queen is my agent, and she pushed and prodded and got this out of me, then placed it with a great publisher. She is a good friend and trusted adviser, and if you don't like this book, take it up with her. Warning: She is at me already for the next book.

◙ Judith McCarthy and the wonderful team at McGraw-Hill—Ron Martirano, Gayathri Vinay, Ann Pryor, and all the great folks in sales and publicity—believed in the book and the message, and that is why you have it.

Now, the course. So many people have helped in so many ways, and they were acknowledged in my previous book. The universe keeps providing amazing individuals who are an ongoing part of my life, and I am grateful:

◙ My new teaching assistants in London—Adam Morris, Anu Sundaram, and Nick Wai—are all wonderful people, and they put up with my foibles and never complain. Adam, in particular, smiles sweetly as he helps me with my computer issues, of which I have many.

◙ My new teaching assistants in New York—Adam Walsh, Marilyn McLeod, Laura Garnett, and Adam Morris—are also great people, and in case you're wondering, it is the same Adam Morris. He wanted to be mentioned twice, so he hopped on a plane and crossed the pond.

◙ My new teaching assistants in California—Brandon Peele and Samir Ghosh—did it once and are ready to do it again, so I guess they are certifiably crazy, but I love them.

◙ Apoorva Ajmera courteously maintains my website (http://areyoureadytosucceed.com) as a labor of love because he believes in what I do and wants to be a part of it.

◨ And last, but by no means least, to all the many brave souls who took my course, told others about it, wrote about it, gave me suggestions for how to improve it, and still have dialogues with me and each other—thank you from the bottom of my heart. You are the people for whom this book was written.

1

What you need
is a paradigm shift

◙

A T CERTAIN MILESTONES—the two most common being birthdays and New Year's Day—people decide that their lives will be different from that day on. I bet this is true of you. At different times, you've probably resolved to eat healthy, exercise regularly, stop procrastinating, catch up on your backlog, stop watching junk TV, get enough sleep, and so on. How long did it last? Odds are you were back to your old habits in short order until the next milestone, when you repeated the cycle again. And again.

There is a reason for this. When you try to bring about behavioral change by an effort of will, you actually do violence to yourself, and the chances are very good that you will not succeed. This is so universally true that you can actually make money from it. Gyms cheerfully and unabashedly sign up many times more members than they can handle in early

January. They know there will be open slots on treadmill sign-up sheets by February.

If you have a strong will and persist in your new behavior, you will likely encounter side effects you would rather not deal with. If you stop smoking cold turkey, you may eat too much and put on weight. Then you starve yourself to regain your ideal body weight, and your crotchety temper ruins relations with your family.

Violence to yourself is not a good way to go.

My methods produce lasting behavioral change without unpleasant consequences, because the change does not come from an effort of will. It comes from examining your deep-rooted beliefs of who you are and how the world functions. As you examine these beliefs and make changes in them, you literally *become* a different person.

And once you're a different person, you behave differently and change happens naturally and effortlessly. Best of all, it lasts. You don't have to worry about sliding back.

When you change enough of your beliefs about "this is the way the world works," the cumulative effect is massive. You will find your own tipping point on this. When you do, you will experience a paradigm shift in which you'll see the world so differently that nothing is the same again. We are not talking about putting a Band-Aid on a cut. We are talking about genetic re-engineering on a massive scale.

This book is designed to help you bring about such a paradigm shift. The chapters are short, but the lessons are powerful. The shift in your consciousness will happen only if you *do* the exercises provided.

To illustrate the power of a paradigm shift, consider this ancient parable:

═══

The abbot of a once-famous Buddhist monastery that had fallen into decline was deeply troubled. Monks were lax in their practice, novices were leaving, and lay supporters were deserting to other centers. He traveled far to see a sage and recounted his tale of woe, saying how much he wanted to transform his monastery to the flourishing haven it had been in days of yore. The sage looked him in the eye and said, "The reason your monastery has languished is that the Buddha is living among you in disguise, and you have not honored Him."

The abbot hurried back, his mind in turmoil. The Selfless One was at his monastery! Who could He be? Brother Hua? No, he was full of sloth. Brother Po? No, he was too dull. But then the Tathagata was in disguise. What better disguise than sloth or dull-wittedness? He called his monks together and revealed the sage's words. They too were taken aback and looked at each other with suspicion and awe. Which one of them was the Chosen One? The disguise was perfect. Not knowing who He was, they took to treating everyone with the respect due the Buddha. Their faces started shining with an inner radiance that attracted novices and then lay supporters. In no time at all, the monastery far surpassed its previous glory.

═══

That is how it works, and you can begin harnessing this power. Right now.

Have you ever been driving to an appointment in heavy traffic when someone cuts in front of you and nearly causes an accident? Then you watch as this person continues to weave through traffic, instigating many near misses and angry honks?

What do you feel? A hot flush of rage? Surging blood pressure? A need for spontaneous profanity? Do you give the offender the finger—or want to? Road rage has caused heart attacks and led to murderous assaults. *Not* a pleasant feeling.

Now imagine this: The person in that car has just received news that his son was involved in an accident and is seriously injured. He is trying desperately to get to the hospital before surgery begins and is crying as he contemplates the real possibility that he may never see his son alive again.

Now how do you feel? Do you experience a gush of sympathy? Do you wish a fellow human being well and send thoughts of strength and goodwill?

You don't know whether that person is an ill-mannered jerk or a distraught parent. Quite likely you will never know. And it doesn't matter. What matters is that *you* get to choose the emotional space you occupy when you contemplate what happens to you. You probably didn't realize you have that choice, but you do.

And by the way, you don't expose yourself to the risk of suffering an accident. If you see the same car again later, you expect erratic behavior and are on guard against it. You just don't have the emotional garbage of rage and dislike.

Think of how many times in your life you have had such a choice and voluntarily decided to occupy a room with anger, frustration, jealousy, or hate. It happens much more often than you realize.

▣

how to choose your emotional state

Whenever anyone does something that causes you to react with anger or distaste, take a deep breath and pause. Think about whether there is any possibility that what set you off was actually a well-meaning act or an honest mistake.

It does *not* matter whether your instincts were accurate or not. The mere act of considering whether there was a more benevolent explanation for what happened is enough to dissipate the violent emotions that bedevil you. You will be more calm and deliberate, and your actions will be more effective.

▣

2

Don't stick a label on it!

THERE IS SOMETHING you do that hurts you a great deal, and you don't even realize you do it. If someone points it out to you, your tendency is to deny it. Even if you acknowledge it, you don't feel particularly troubled. It seems innocuous. Everyone does it. In fact, doing it is embedded into our culture.

What is it that is so common and so deleterious?

It is your habit of making instantaneous judgments about everything and then sticking a label on whatever happens. In particular, I am talking about the labels "good thing" and "bad thing."

Observe yourself as you go through a typical day. Stuff happens to you. As it does, you immediately judge it and label it. Dozens of times. Hundreds of times. So often that you no longer recognize that you're doing it. It is a deep-seated habit. Consider these fairly typical situations:

- ▣ You go to the coffee machine, and only the dregs of the previous pot are left. If you want fresh coffee, you have to clean the pot and brew it. ("bad thing")

- ▣ Your assistant calls. Her son is ill, and she has to take him to the doctor. She expects to be in but can't say when. ("bad thing")

- ▣ There's an unexpected crisis in Asia, and your boss has to leave immediately to sort it out. Your meeting with him, which took two months to set up, is canceled. ("bad thing")

- ▣ The canceled meeting means the report you're working on doesn't really have to be completed by the end of the week. ("good thing")

- ▣ You get a voice mail from your biggest customer. She wants you to call her back immediately. What could she want? ("probable bad thing")

- ▣ Your hard drive crashes, erasing the document you were working on. ("bad thing")

- ▣ The tech guys say that the crash is pretty complete, and they can't recover the files for you. It costs several hundred dollars to send it out to a forensic PC specialist who may or may not be able to help. ("bad thing")

- ▣ The PC specialist can recover about half the files on your hard drive. The ones you really need are in this set. ("good thing")

- ▣ Your new PC is set up so that all your files are automatically backed up every night. The most you can lose in the future is one day's work. ("good thing")

▣ You learn that your company's CEO called to set up an extended meeting with your colleague. You haven't heard from him, even though you've left a message. One of the two of you will be promoted. ("*very* bad thing")

▣ You receive a six-figure bonus. ("*very* good thing")

▣ Your teammate, the one you dislike, gets a seven-figure bonus. ("*very* bad thing" that makes your own bonus slide down from "very good thing" to "OK thing")

▣ You get a call from your spouse. Your in-laws are coming for dinner on Friday and may stay the weekend. ("bad thing, very bad thing, super bad thing")

▣ Your daughter's SAT scores came in; she got 2390. ("good thing")

▣ If she hadn't flubbed that simple math question, she would have had a perfect score. ("bad thing")

▣ Your doctor calls. Nothing to be alarmed about, but he would like to rerun some tests. What does he mean, nothing to be alarmed about? What tests? Why does he want to do them over? ("*very* bad thing")

And so it goes on, minute by minute, day after day. Most people use the "bad thing" label three to ten times more often than they use the "good thing" label.

Each time you use the "bad thing" label, no matter how fleetingly, you're adding a tiny bit of stress to your life. You may think that's trivial. It isn't. You may even claim that it has no effect on you. You're wrong. Cumulatively, it has a *huge* impact on you.

When you label so much of what happens to you as "bad," it reinforces the feeling that you are a powerless pawn at the mercy of outside forces over which you have no control. And—this is key—labeling something a bad thing almost guarantees that you'll experience it as such.

If you look back on your life, you'll find many instances where something you labeled a bad thing turned out to be not so bad after all and perhaps even a good thing. Such as the time you called everyone over for a football party and your TV blew, so you played charades instead, and everyone had a complete blast. Here is a perfect example of how difficult it is to know immediately whether something is good or bad.

===

He was a good swimmer, a very good swimmer, and was training to compete in an important meet. He slipped on a patch of ice and broke his wrist. For weeks and weeks his coach kept him on the sidelines kicking, while his teammates practiced furiously. Initially, he was devastated and felt that his career was over. Then he simply buckled down to doing what his coach told him to do.

At the meet, in one of the crucial events, his opponent swam the race of his life. He was quite behind at the halfway mark and should have lost. But the weeks of kicking had given him muscles he'd never had before. He kicked even harder and touched the finish wall a whisker before his inspired opponent.

===

The swimmer was Michael Phelps. The event was the 100-meter butterfly in the 2008 Beijing Olympics. He beat Milorad Cavic by $\frac{1}{100}$ th of a second to win his seventh gold medal. Frame-by-frame photographs showed a tired Cavic gliding with his legs trailing while Phelps gave a final kick. It was one of the closest finishes in athletic history. And without that extra spurt, Phelps would not have won eight gold medals in a single Olympics to beat Mark Spitz's record.

So when Phelps broke his wrist in the midst of his most intense training, was it a bad thing or a good thing? Who knows? A case can certainly be made that that injury was the best thing that ever happened to him.

▣

how to stop using unhelpful labels

Observe yourself closely. Notice how you immediately judge what happens to you and label it a bad thing or a good thing. Focus on the bad things. See the many ways in which they are not so bad and perhaps even good.

Even if you can't see how something can possibly be good, refrain from labeling it "bad." If you break your leg, don't label it a bad thing. If you have to stick a label on it, use "I broke my leg." This is descriptive and neutral. Be generous with the "good thing" label.

It may take you a while to get the hang of it and even to recognize how many judgments you pass. Persist.

See how your life changes when you stop using the "bad thing" label.

▣

3

Why positive thinking is bad for you

▣

O K, I USED A LITTLE bit of license here. Positive thinking is not really bad for you. It's simply not as effective
as something else I will show you.

Imagine you're in a hurry, in the lobby of a tall building,
and you have to get to the top floor. Positive thinking will
have you run up the stairs with a resolute heart and unflagging
determination. Your legs pump and your muscles ache, but
you keep going. You'll eventually get to the top, but it will
take longer than you want it to and you'll be exhausted when
you get there.

With my method, you simply take the express elevator.
You'll get to the top faster and find yourself fresher and better
able to take care of whatever business you have.

What is the method I advocate? I'll tell you in Chapter 4,
but first let me explain why positive thinking is an inadequate
strategy.

"Positive thinking" is embedded in our national psyche as an appropriate response to the curveballs life throws us. Parents and relatives urge us to "think positive" and "look on the bright side" when we're down. Doubtless more than one person has told you to "make lemonade when life gives you lemons." Well-wishers say that "the darkest hour is before the dawn."

They're all correct. But you don't realize that, by doing what they suggest, you are effectively taking a car with eight cylinders and disabling four of them. Sure, the four working cylinders will still take you where you want to go, but you have given up a lot of the power and speed.

Don't get me wrong. I readily concede that positive thinking has benefited many people. It has enabled them to kick destructive addictions; get derailed lives back on track; recover from financial setbacks, relationship breakups, and similar disasters; and cope better with the vicissitudes of life. But there is still a problem with it.

The problem is that it sets up a duality and encourages you to embrace only one part of it. This duality is embedded in the name itself. If you embrace "positive thinking," you are—by definition—spurning "negative thinking." So it's as if you were on a teeter-totter and are trying desperately to put all your weight on one side—the "positive thinking" side. You have to muster all your energy and throw it into weighing down the "positive" side because you are scared deep down that the "negative" side you've created is quite strong and may actually "win" this battle. This creates stress. And there will be many occasions when you don't succeed.

Think of how this duality permeates all the well-meaning advice you're given. When you look on the bright side, you're acknowledging that there is a dark side at which you are choosing not to gaze. If you think that the darkest hour is before the dawn, you accept that you are moving from darkness to light.

To a certain extent, you're kidding yourself. To a large extent, you're dissipating your mental energy to overcome an obstacle that you've created yourself. You created this barrier by labeling somthing as "undesirable." You then tried to see the best aspect of this "undesirable" thing. You're much better off using that energy and focusing it on the task you're engaged in. You don't have to dissipate your vitality overcoming "bad" things if you don't label them "bad" in the first place.

Consider a mouse in a laboratory maze looking for cheese. It takes a wrong turn and bumps into a dead end, promptly turns around, and tries another route. And another and another, until it gets to the cheese. Now imagine what would happen if every third time it reached a blind alley it had to sit down and recharge itself. If it had to convince itself that the cheese was there. That it had to try harder and not take failures into account. That the dark days would turn to light when it found the cheese. That the "bad thing" of yet another dead end was actually the "good thing" of greater knowledge of maze pathways.

Don't laugh. You can readily appreciate—when it's presented this way—that the mouse strategy of simply getting on with it is superior to using positive thinking.

This is equally true for you. Even if you don't recognize it, you have already taken the first step on this path. You started when you did the exercise in the last chapter and began avoiding putting labels on stuff that happens to you. Especially when you avoid putting the "bad thing" label on whatever you confront.

Reflect on this: You need to "think positive" when a "bad thing" happens to you. This takes energy and causes tension. It creates a tiny bit of stress, even as it dissipates the much larger stress caused by the "bad thing."

But what if no "bad thing" happens to you because you refuse to use that label? You no longer have to put a positive spin on whatever life gives you. Others may think of events as "bad" or even "terrible," but you don't have to let them dictate what you experience. You can choose for yourself, calmly and deliberately. Then you don't need to marshal your resources and "think positive." You just do what you have to. It's much more effective.

◙

you don't need to "think positive"
if you don't use the "bad thing" label

Continue to eschew using the "bad thing" label when events don't go the way you would prefer. Visualize a chess-playing computer. When it makes an error, it simply notes it. There is no anguish, no beating up on itself. Even when it makes a blunder and loses a piece, it simply carries on. When the opponent makes a strong move, there is no fear, no depth of despair. When IBM's Deep Blue defeated reigning chess champion Gary Kasparov in 1997, Kasparov mentioned that he was unable to demoralize it as he had so many of his human opponents. In fact, his inability to intimidate Deep Blue actually demoralized *him*.

Try to be like Deep Blue as you go through your day. Simply observe whatever happens to you, but do not get emotionally swayed. Do what you have to, but don't surrender your calmness and sense of peace. The bad news is that you will not succeed. The good news is that even a slight move in that direction will hugely improve your life.

◙

4

Be a Daruma doll

▣

DESPITE THE TITLE, what I actually stated in Chapter 3 was that while positive thinking is widely lauded and may have helped many, there is an approach to life that is far superior. That approach is *extreme resilience.*

Resilience is the ability of a material to return to its original form or position after being bent, compressed, or stretched. In common parlance, it is the ability to recover from adversity.

Resilience is just on the cusp of becoming the new management fad, and articles on it have started appearing in peer-reviewed journals. Leadership programs have begun talking about how important it is and how to cultivate it.

I sincerely hope that this is one trend that does not disappear as other fads have. Resilience is a powerful tool in your arsenal. Extreme resilience is even better.

With extreme resilience, you recover so fast that, to an outside observer, it does not seem as if you were laid low at all. So fast that you yourself are not aware of having gone through the cycle of misfortune and snapping back. Quite possibly, if you have become adept at not using the "bad thing" label, you never go through the cycle at all.

Have you ever seen a Daruma doll? It is patterned after Bodhidharma, the patriarch of Zen Buddhism. Legend has it that Bodhidharma meditated so fiercely in a mountain cave that his arms and legs atrophied and fell off. He subsequently became enlightened and is now a revered figure, credited with spreading Buddhism through China into Japan.

A Daruma doll is armless and legless and has a wide, heavily weighted bottom. Knock it down, and it instantly springs up. Flatten it ten times, and it springs up ten times. As you pull back your hand after knocking it over, it is already upright or on the way. You can't keep a Daruma doll down. And it's also a talisman of good luck.

Think of the implications of being like a Daruma doll. You spend entirely too much time coping with the misfortunes that afflict you. It's good to be resilient, because after a short while you get back on your feet. But that short while is still wasted time and is not a pleasant interval. How about shortening that interval or making it disappear entirely?

Have you ever watched an infant learn to walk? It usually happens somewhere around eleven to thirteen months. The baby stands up and tries to imitate adults she has seen to take a step. She falls down and bawls. Mommy or daddy rushes to comfort her. This happens a few times. Soon she forgets to cry. When she falls, she simply picks herself up and stands again. When she takes a tottering step and remains upright, a beatific smile appears on her face. She pitches over, gets herself upright, and tries again. Soon—generally in less than a day—she is staggering around, upsetting the living room arrangements and requiring a whole new stage of parenting.

Now imagine what would happen if, each time she stumbled, she had to fight feelings of despair about whether she would ever be able to learn to walk. If she castigated herself for being a failure because she still had not mastered something that others did effortlessly. If she needed time and counseling to recover from the tragedy of each fall. How long would it take her to learn to walk then?

You do exactly that in your life. You spend much time in needless, fruitless self-recrimination and blaming others. You go on pointless guilt trips and make excuses that you know are fatuous. If you're resilient, you recover and go on to do great things.

How about adopting extreme resilience and going on to do even greater things? Many hugely successful businesspersons have been extremely resilient.

===

He was a young man of twenty-one when he came to the great city. He became a clerk at a dry goods store and worked his way up. He partnered with a bookkeeper, and both became junior partners in the firm. When the senior partner, plagued by ailing health, wanted to retire, the two went into debt and acquired the company.

It flourished under their management. One day, the city caught fire, and their store went up in flames. Insurance covered only a fraction of the goods. Even before the flames had died down, the former clerk was planning to rebuild on a bigger scale. He quickly organized a rescue squad to save as much of the merchandise as possible and opened a temporary store nearby. Within a year, he had returned to the same location with a new five-story store. Soon he bought out his partner.

Six years later, that store caught fire and was leveled. Undaunted, he planned an even grander establishment as he watched his emporium disappear. Within a month, he had reopened in a lakefront exposition hall leased from the city. In less than two years, he was back with a six-story edifice that became a national landmark.

He was a retailing pioneer—the first to open a tearoom in a department store, the first to offer revolving credit to customers, the first to use escalators. At his death, he was one of the richest men in the nation, a noted philanthropist and pillar of society.

=====

The man was Marshall Field. His first store was destroyed in the Chicago fire of 1871, and the replacement caught fire and burnt down in 1877. That State Street store's Christmas windows, restaurants, and Frango mints are still the stuff of retailing legend.

Can you develop extreme resilience? Absolutely! Do the exercises in this book conscientiously. As you become comfortable with them, you will automatically look at the world differently and extreme resilience will become "normal" for you.

▣

how to cultivate extreme resilience

Imagine you're a civil engineer called to build a road through difficult terrain. You notice loose shale, a granite mountain that lies squarely in the way of the proposed road, marshy ground, and so on. You don't rail against any of these obstacles. They are simply the constraints that you have to accommodate. Your genius lies in accomplishing your objectives even though you're hampered. The challenge itself is exhilarating.

Cultivate this attitude in real time. Your store burning down is merely giving you the opportunity to build a bigger, better one. Try it.

▣

5

Let it go—babies do!!

□

M ANY YEARS AGO, when I was a student and still new
to the United States, a friend suggested we take a long
hike in the woods. It was a gorgeous summer day, and I
jumped at the thought of escaping the concrete jungle I was
in. Reading a novel under a tree by a lake seemed just what
the doctor ordered to combat loneliness and homesickness.

It took me five minutes to get ready. I had some leftover
eggplant parmigiana in the fridge. I didn't have aluminum
foil, so I took the casserole dish. I skipped the light, disposable,
Tetra pack with apple juice in favor of root beer in a glass
bottle. I thought my buddy might like one, so I took one for
him. I was almost at the end of a gripping thriller, and next up
was a historical novel spanning two continents and a hundred
years. I took both, even though they were hardbacks and the
significance of this eluded me. I couldn't get everything I
needed into my backpack, so I put the leftover stuff in a plastic
bag. No sweat. It didn't weigh all that much.

We drove upstate from Manhattan for a while, parked, and headed out into the forest. The first two hours were just fine. We had an enjoyable late lunch. I didn't want to litter, so I put the empty root beer bottles back in my pack, and we set out again. It was not so fine after that. My shoulders ached. My arms felt as if they were dropping off.

Finally, I discarded my inhibitions about littering along with the root beer bottles. I found out "who did it" in the thriller because I finished it after lunch, but I never discovered why the upright, aristocratic family disintegrated after two generations; I paid a fine for both "lost" books. And somewhere in the Adirondacks, a four-hour hike from the I-95, nestled in the hollow of an evergreen's roots, is a white casserole dish with a bright blue flower motif.

I understand why experienced hikers pay hundreds of dollars for super-strong, lightweight rope and a tent that weighs a pound less than another brand. You don't want to carry any extra stuff on a long journey when you're on your own. The manager of the space shuttle program cheerfully forks out tens of thousands of dollars to lop a few ounces off the payload and considers it money well spent.

You too are on a long journey and are on your own. It is called life. You came into it alone, you will depart it alone, and in between—even though you may be surrounded by others—you are essentially alone.

The mental detritus that you insist on carrying around on this journey is every bit as enervating and debilitating as the physical stuff that slows you down on a long hike.

A marriage counselor I know was speaking about the reasons couples split up. "The number-one reason they are unable to come to terms is that they never let go," he explained. The wife remembers in startling detail, including dates and times, all the sarcastic remarks her mother-in-law has made. She cites all the times her husband has forgotten birthdays, spoken slightingly of her friends, disparaged her efforts to beautify their home. The husband recalls, equally accurately, the number of times she has prevented him from going to a game he really wanted to see, the friends she froze out of his life, and the numerous occasions she "had a headache." "Crap happens in every relationship," the counselor went on. "The ones who survive are the ones who can drop it, clean up, and move on."

You also are carrying heavy burdens, and the odds are quite good that you don't even recognize it. Is there a colleague at work whose presence fills you with distaste and a feeling of dread? Do you find yourself reacting viscerally to a relative? Do you "know" that a meeting your boss has called is going to be a total waste of time? Are there people who rub you the wrong way, social situations that make you uneasy, tasks that bore you to death?

If you answered "yes" to any of these questions, then you're bowing under the weight of your load.

"Whoa!" I hear you say. "This is just knowledge. I didn't create this stuff. I merely recognized it." This is a common reaction. A jerk is a jerk. When you have had many experiences of the "jerkiness" of an individual at work, it is easy to label him a jerk and treat him as such.

But I am not really concerned with that individual. I don't even care whether he is or is not a jerk. What matters is the feeling you have toward him. The groaning expectation when you meet him that the interaction will be distasteful. The dread you feel beforehand. *That* is the burden you carry. That is the sum total of the experience that you have not let go.

It is possible that at least some of that person's "jerkiness" comes from the prison in which you're holding him—and yourself. The Pygmalion effect has been well documented. In one study, teachers who were told that randomly selected students were "very bright" developed expectations that those students would perform at high levels. Lo and behold, they did far better than their peers. Other researchers have found similar effects in a variety of settings. Your expectations do affect the outcome you observe.

Watch a baby gurgling happily and chugging milk from his bottle. Now take the bottle away. He screws up his face and bawls. He turns red. There is no doubt at all that he is *really* angry. Now give his bottle back. In seconds, he is back to a state of contentment as he drains the bottle.

Babies know how to let things go. When they are angry, they are angry. When they are sad, they are sad. When they are finished playing with a toy, they are done with it. They don't carry anything around. Each thing that happens to them is something new to be experienced in the moment.

Your problem is that you carry stuff around. Over time, the accumulation becomes burdensome indeed. Drop it.

▣

drop the useless baggage you carry around

Are there troublesome people in your life? The next time you meet one, forget the history. Don't expect that the interaction will be unpleasant. Expect that it will be delightful, and if it isn't, then let it go. Don't carry it over to the next time you meet.

Do the same with unpleasant situations. Note how many times your existing expectations sour your experience. Consciously drop the past. It's hard, but with practice, you will get the hang of it.

▣

6

Think your problem is managing time? It's *not*!!!

▣

I ONCE SPOKE TO an audience of about fifty. Every single person present was a CEO and ran his or her company's operations in a specific country. Quite a few handled multiple countries. Collectively, they were responsible for sales of several billion dollars. Many came up to me after my presentation and confessed that they had a problem managing their time. They wanted to do better and needed some help.

Another time, I spoke to an audience of several hundred MBAs and soon-to-be MBAs at a top business school. Many came up to me afterward and confessed that they had a problem managing their time. They wanted to do better and needed some help.

I also spoke to an eclectic audience comprising everyone from trapeze artists to Wall Street titans. Many came up to me afterward and confessed that they had a problem managing their time. They wanted to do better and needed some help.

You're probably nodding your head in agreement. You too may think that you need to manage your time more effectively and are looking for ways to do so.

Let me put it bluntly: You *don't* need to manage your time better. You *can't* manage your time better. There is *nothing* you can do to manage your time better.

You, me, the neighbor down the street you don't like, and your daughter who is always behind on everything—we each get twenty-four hours a day. Each hour has sixty minutes, and each minute has sixty seconds. By the time you have finished reading this, you have used up ninety of those seconds.

If you're pious and altruistic and spend all your time helping out at soup kitchens, you don't get a few seconds more. If you're a sadistic serial killer, you don't get a few seconds less. That's just the way it is. (I know, I know. The stuff of time does alter in different states of consciousness, but that's not what we're talking about now.)

Remember the paradigm shifts we talked about in Chapter 1? This is one: You don't need to manage time better. You need to manage yourself better.

Time is something outside yourself. You can't be held responsible for it. It is much easier to place the blame for failure on this external thing. Not being a good "time manager" is an easy psychological cop-out.

But not being able to manage yourself? Now that is serious. It's not something you can sweep under the carpet. It's something that you have to grapple with and fix. What will your friends, your family, your colleagues, and your bosses think of you if you have a problem managing yourself? Can you even afford to let them know?

I doubt that you have a problem going up to a consultant and revealing that you need help managing your time. Perhaps you already have. Would you go up to the same person and confess that you need help managing yourself? Why not? You *do* need such help!

⸻

The alarm rudely woke Alice. She was in the middle of an uneasy dream—not a nightmare, but unpleasant. For a moment she could not remember where she was, and then memory came flooding back. Her report was due today at 5:00 P.M. She should have finished it by now, but her college roommate had been in town for two nights, and they'd had so much to catch up on. Her head ached. Maybe she shouldn't have had that fourth glass of wine—or the fifth.

She was late for work. She nicked herself shaving her legs. It was a deep gash and opened up again when she put on her dress. She put a cotton ball on it held in place with a bandage. Ditching her dress, she wore a pantsuit instead.

She rushed to her office and booted her PC. She tried to retrieve the document that she was working on. The screen impersonally told her that she had performed an illegal operation and it would now close. It did so. Drat. She had been having this problem for a while and had meant to have the tech guys look at it.

Walking outside, she asked her secretary to use her office and seated herself at the secretary's desk. She pulled up the report. There was a ping telling her that an e-mail had just come in. It was her secretary's PC, but the e-mail was for her. Her boss needed a file on a current project right away. She had known that her boss would need it and had planned last week to have it updated and ready. Somehow she'd forgotten. That had been the evening they'd all gone bowling after work. Darn. She had ten minutes to make the necessary changes before walking the file up to her boss—not enough time. She decided to tell her boss what she intended to put in her memo. Nowhere as effective as giving him the finished memo but the best she could do at the moment.

She came back to find her girlfriend from purchasing in her office. Would she like to have lunch? Sure, why not. Gotta eat. She had a martini—just one. It was relaxing. When she got back to the office, she was mellow. Too mellow. She just couldn't concentrate on the report. She finished it somehow and handed it in to the martinet on the top floor—the one who made sure that time-sensitive documents got to the right people.

She was almost home when she remembered that she had forgotten to include a key section on valuations. This had been done by the new person in banking, and she had received it a week ago. She rushed back to the office, retrieved the missing section, and went back to the top floor. The martinet was still there and accepted it gracelessly.

She was tired, dead tired. Maybe she could stop by her favorite bar on the way home. She really needed a drink.

═══

Does Alice need to manage time? Or herself? What about you?

▣

begin managing yourself and more time will magically appear

Observe yourself as you go through the day. How often do you start a task only to set it aside as something else grabs your attention—e-mail, Twitter notifications, Facebook requests, instant messages, colleagues dropping in? Try turning off your cell phone and shutting down the communication functions on your PC unless you absolutely need to be connected. Many of the distractions that sap your energy just disappear. This will drive home that you don't really have a problem managing time. You do have a huge problem managing yourself. Many of the exercises in later chapters address this issue more specifically.

▣

7

What do you really do (part 1)?

▣

M Y VISION FOR you is that you are so energized by what you do that you find yourself quivering with anticipation at the thought of going to work. That Monday morning is something you look forward to with great eagerness. That you derive deep meaning and sustenance from your labors and that this satisfaction increases with each passing day.

Imagine this: A senior executive in your organization calls you to an urgent meeting in his office. Times are bad. Sales are down. Business prospects are uncertain. Lots of people are being let go. The good news is that you will be retained. The bad news is that your pay will be cut in half.

Sit back for a moment and really consider this situation. Make it as vivid and real as you possibly can. Then evaluate your instinctual reaction. What immediately flashes through your mind? Is it "That's it! I'm outta here. Tonight I polish my résumé, tomorrow I start circulating it discreetly, and in three weeks to two months I'll be gone"? Or is it "That's really too bad! What do I have to do to manage with my reduced compensation, and what can I do to make my organization prosperous again so I can get back to where I was and even surpass it?"

If your reaction is the former, you're wasting your life. If you're ready to leave where you are instantly and the only thing holding you back is a paycheck, then you're paying a psychic cost that is too high. If your remuneration is normally outrageous, as it frequently is in the financial services industry, you may be tempted to hold on in the hope that a few years of perdition will free you forever. Perhaps this strategy will work for you, but remember that it is equally likely your stint in such surroundings will warp you in unforeseen ways and leave you tethered to an ever-faster treadmill.

If your reaction is the latter, then you have much to be grateful for and you're not too far from the vision I described. Odds are that you're somewhere in between, and that's a good sign that you should start moving in the direction of greater engagement.

How do you begin such movement? This instructive tale answers that question.

===

In the Middle Ages, there was a famine in the countryside, so the young men went to the city to make a living. Three of them—John, Peter, and Paul—were from the same village, and they all found employment in the house-cum-studio of a great artist. They had not known each other before. The artist also had roots in their village, which was why he hired them out of the many hundreds who besieged him for any job at any wage—some even willing to work for scraps of food and a place to sleep.

The artist had risen from humble beginnings because of a combination of talent, luck, and hard work. Now he was famous across the continent, and even the Pope beseeched him to paint the murals in a great cathedral. He was resting at home and intended to take up that job when he was done with some paintings for which he had been commissioned.

He set the three youths to work immediately, and the hours were long. He bought small stones from travelers from distant countries in the East, and the young men were required to crush them with hammers until they became a fine powder, then soak the powder in a foul-smelling liquid, then drain and evaporate the liquid on sheets of muslin. He also gave them samples of plants and sent them out to distant hills to gather great quantities. They then had to crush the plants and boil the juice into a concentrate. From all this came pigments of rich color that the artist used in his work. He was creating a stockpile of materials he would need for the murals.

John disliked the work, the smell, and the hours and only remained because he saw no alternative. Peter did not particularly like what he did, but he thought it was better than the hard labor that was the lot of a friend who worked at the blacksmith's foundry, so he diligently did what he was supposed to do. Paul was intrigued by the iridescent colors that appeared from humdrum sources as if by magic and began to experiment. He paid attention to what the artist said, observed him at work, and asked questions. When he was not rebuffed, he felt encouraged and began asking questions regularly. That is how he knew the artist was looking for a particular shade of red, and he saw a plant that he thought would yield such a hue when its juice was mixed with another, which turned out to be the case. The artist was mightily pleased.

When his commissions were finished, the artist wound up his establishment. John was dismissed. Peter was paid a small stipend— barely enough to keep body and soul together—to help maintain the house and keep it in good repair. As for Paul, the artist asked him if he would like to accompany him and be his apprentice. Paul accepted joyfully and, in time, became a noted artist in his own right.

═══

This, in a sense, is the choice you have every day. You can be, in the words of George Bernard Shaw, "a feverish, selfish little clod of ailments and grievances complaining that the world will not devote itself to making you happy," or you can be an eagle soaring effortlessly in the sun. You can be John, essentially a laborer for hire. You can be Peter, essentially an industrious craftsman. Or you can be Paul, an eager creator of beauty who is curious about the world and actively engaged with it in a quest to make it better. Choose wisely.

◙

make it a game, and unpleasant situations will no longer faze you

There are many things you have to do in life that you find distasteful—meet with disagreeable clients, have dinner with in-laws you dislike, discipline wayward children, and so on. Observe your emotions as you perform such activities. Note how often you feel self-pity and resentment. Now recognize that you can wallow in these negative feelings, or you can simply let them go. And you *can* let them go. Make it a game or many games. See how long you can carry on a conversation with the person you dislike without making a sarcastic comment. How many times does the self-important, pompous client use the word *I* in a five-minute span? Concentrate quietly on playing your game, and the unpleasantness melts away.

◙

8

What do you really do (part 2)?

▣

THE VISION I laid out for you in Chapter 7 about being so engaged in what you do that you cannot wait to get to work is a powerful one. *Everyone* wants to be there. I have heard thousands of confessions along the lines of "What you say really makes sense to me, Professor Rao. The problem is that nothing really calls to me in the way you describe. I mean, I like my job, but it's just a job. I certainly don't go into rhapsodies over it, and there are many times I actually find it distasteful. I'm happy—most of the time, anyway. Not ecstatic, but satisfied. How do I get to what you're talking about?" It is possible, indeed likely, that you feel this way.

I ask people to describe their ideal job, one that would make them come alive, that they would feel passionate about. They begin excitedly. They specify how much it would pay, where it would be located, how much travel it would involve, the type of person their boss would be, the culture of the organization, the nature of the work they would do, what the hours would be and how much flexibility they would have, their prospects of moving up, and so on. A very few also specify what good their work would bring to the world.

All are convinced that their ideal job is "out there" and their task is to find it. Do you think the same way? That if only you could find this specified set of characteristics you would be passionate about what you do and fulfilled in your work?

If you believe this and are seeking such a position, sometimes desultorily, sometimes actively, then I have some bad news for you. You are *wrong*! First, the exact combination of attributes you are looking for does not exist in any job. Second, even if, by some miracle, it did exist and you could find it, it would be no more than a few months before you were as sick and miserable in it as you are right now.

Here is an immutable truth for you to ponder: Passion does not exist in the job. It exists in you—and if you cannot ignite it within yourself right where you are now, you will never find it outside yourself. It is futile to search frenetically for that perfect position. Paradoxically, when you discover the truth of this and begin to kindle the blaze within yourself, the external world rearranges itself to bring you what you seek and usually much faster than you expected.

Consider this classic immigrant story:

Joey came to his new country with many handicaps. He did not know the language. He did not understand the culture. He had no money and no friends or relatives to rely on. He missed the food and the music and the fellowship of his homeland.

He gritted his teeth and got a menial job washing dishes in a road-side diner. Twenty years later, he owned a string of eating places in three states and was very well-to-do. And his family? They were all with him in his large, well-appointed home or nearby in other homes they had built or bought. He anchored the bridge they all crossed into a strange land where they set down roots and flourished.

═══

You have certainly heard some variant of this story and may even know someone who is like Joey. How and why did he make good—and so decisively? The answer is simple, and you already know it. Joey was never really washing dishes or doing menial tasks. When he was washing dishes, he was actually helping his kids get an education and enabling them to build a life far better than he could ever have conceived for himself. That is what kept him going and provided the fuel his rocket used to take off.

What do you do in your job? Take five minutes and write it down. Do it now.

Now look at what you've written. If you have described what you do in functional terms, such as "I make pro forma balance sheets and income statements and reconcile them," "I devise marketing strategies for new products," or "I sell widgets to companies that are in the energy business," then you are burnt out or on the way to being burnt out.

If you see what you do as a set of functions, then you're taking a six-inch view, and when you travel the road of life with your nose six inches from the ground, it gets plenty abraded. Soar like an eagle and take a ten-thousand-foot view.

Do you, perchance, work in the accounting department of a large pharmaceutical firm? Then consider this: A beautiful woman was in a terrible accident. Her face went through the windshield, and there were lots of glass fragments embedded in the jagged tears in her skin. The sutures your company makes were used by the plastic surgeon to help her get her beauty back. In another case, a middle-aged father suffered a heart attack. The stent your company makes gave him a chance to live a normal life again. It is not enough for you to know all this intellectually. You have to feel it at a very deep level. You are part of an organization that helps distressed people in significant ways. This is the reason you get up in the morning and go to work—not to add up numbers in columns and make sure they balance.

▣

change your story about what you do

What products and services does your company provide? How do they benefit the ultimate customer? Make a list of these benefits. Go out and actually visit customers and see them smile. Take a field trip and see the products at work. Know that the lives of tens of thousands of people are improved in some small way because of the company of which you are a part.

▣

It is not always easy to capture this feeling when you are a small part of a large organization and that organization sometimes seems to be frozen in a dysfunctional mode. It is your job to help thaw this dysfunction and help generate movement toward genuine service. This effort is crucial for you. You're doing it for *you*, not for the company, not for your boss, not for your colleagues. Just for you. Do you want to be stuck in a dreary round of meaningless tasks that drive you to utter boredom, or would you like to be the change agent who sparks a movement that energizes everyone else?

As you start out eagerly on this mission, you will run into roadblocks such as people who are unmoving in their lethargy and resistance, uncaring bureaucracy, and lack of resources. Don't let any of them steal your enthusiasm. You *can* remain as fresh and eager as you were on the day you started. Do not let the immensity of the task and the smallness of your successes erode your well-being. You can remain cheerfully upbeat if you invest in the process and not the outcome. Chapter 14 explains this in more detail. The intention and intensity with which you perform your actions has a greater effect on your well-being than what you actually accomplish.

—

In the Indian mythological epic *The Ramayana*, Rama was about to embark on the final battle with the demon Ravana, who had abducted Rama's wife, Sita, and was holding her captive. He had to cross a sea to reach the enemy fortress, and an immense causeway was being constructed.

A squirrel devoted to Rama—who was the epitome of love and goodness and duty—wished to help with the construction. She went to the beach and rubbed her head in the sand, then went to the sea and shook her head so the grains of sand fell off. She did this again and again. The laborers and larger animals who were busy carrying great boulders pointed at her and guffawed, but she persisted.

Rama himself came to see what the fuss was about and was so moved by her devotion that he stroked her head. She instantly became enlightened.

===

That is the choice you have every day. If you are the squirrel and constantly look to see how much of the causeway is coming into being as a result of your toil, and tie your well-being to the success of your efforts, then you will be frustrated and stressed and unhappy. But if you persist in taking your few grains of sand, dropping them into the sea, and relaxing into the knowledge that you are doing the best you can in a worthwhile cause, the task itself will bless you, and you will find joy welling up from within you.

Remember that there is no winning or losing. When you sincerely make the effort, you win every time.

9

What do *you* notice?

◉

HERE IS SOMETHING that most people do and unfortunately never realize it. Sometimes the consequences are painful. It leads to ruptured relationships and even divorce. It holds you back from a promotion and could even cause you to be fired. It prevents you from achieving the goals you set for yourself—being a better parent, losing weight, quitting smoking, becoming a star at work. The really funny thing is that despite the many ways you become frustrated by the results of this single habit, you almost never recognize that you played a central role in creating your misfortune.

Sometimes this habit works in your favor. More often it does not, and the result can be very sad, even traumatic. It is probably the single most important factor in the estrangement between parents and children and between spouses. It has an equally powerful effect on business relationships with subordinates, peers, and bosses.

Are you curious about what this habit is? I thought you might be!

We all think we see the world as it is. We're wrong. We see the world as we are. Let me repeat that: We *never* see the world as it is. We *always* see it as we are.

===

Susan woke up early, as was her wont, and went to the kitchen to make herself a cup of tea. She relished this first cup in the solitude of the early morning. She noticed that there was a plate, as well as a knife and fork, in the sink. Her husband had had a late-night snack.

"Why doesn't he rinse them off and put them in the dishwasher?" she thought angrily. "He knows how much I hate a dirty sink. He just doesn't care." All of her husband's manifest faults, from failing to sort his laundry to watching all the football games, flooded into her head, and she picked up the plate with such force that it struck the faucet and broke. "He just doesn't care," she muttered to herself, and her morning tea did not bring any comfort.

There were still anger lines on her face when she went to work, and she noticed that her assistant had left the draft of a new proposal on her desk. Pages two and three were transposed. She pried the staple loose, rearranged the disordered pages, and stapled it again. "Why doesn't he care enough to do a good job?" she fumed, and called him in to berate him. He was sullen and left work early. When she needed an explanation of an intricate calculation, he was not there, and her boss tartly told her to find out and report back.

She worked late and was just turning into her driveway when she noticed that her neighbor was leaving her front door. He was walking across the lawn to his house, and she scowled. She did not like people walking on the grass, especially not now when the yard was freshly seeded. "Why don't people care?" she seethed.

Susan was a good worker and very diligent, but so many of her colleagues were complaining about her that her boss made her sit down with an executive coach he engaged for her. It was either that or a pink slip.

She accepted with ill humor. "There's nothing wrong with me," she stated flatly. "It's just that I really care about things and they don't." She looked at the coach defiantly. He took detailed notes and said little.

When they met again, the coach had done his homework. "Did you know that your husband has taken on another job?" he queried. "He has a consulting gig with a start-up and hopes to save enough so you can take the Antarctic cruise you always wanted this December. He didn't have time for dinner, so he just grabbed what he found in the fridge and went right off to sleep."

She hadn't known it. She also hadn't known that her assistant had put in an all-nighter so that she would have something in writing before her meeting with her boss or that her neighbor had called to drop off fresh tomatoes from the first batch that ripened in his backyard.

"You are too wedded to the idea that you care and they don't," the coach told her gently. "What you really mean is that they don't always do exactly what you want them to do, and you misinterpret this. If you don't work with me to change your attitude, you may not be with this company much longer." He debated whether to tell her that she might not be married either but decided against it.

=====

Susan thought her finicky demands were a sign of her caring and drive for perfection and saw everyone around her through that narrow lens.

So does this mean that she has to let go of her standards and accept work she considers shoddy? Should she reconcile herself to stacks of dirty dishes in the sink, sloppily put-together presentations, and well-worn paths across her front lawn?

Not at all. It does mean that she has to see each occurrence in context. It emphatically means that she cannot label people based on her limited views. It means that she cannot let others' noncompliance with her demands affect her emotional equanimity. And finally it means that she has to work at achieving a satisfactory compromise with the important people in her life—at home and at work.

The funny thing about life is that the more you expect the best of people and give them room to be themselves without suffocating them with your expectations, the more they will surprise you. The late Carnegie Mellon University professor Randy Pausch got it exactly right when he admonished listeners of his "Last Lecture" to never give up on people because, sooner or later, they will astonish you. Just try this and see for yourself.

◙

you see the world as you are, not as it is

You observe things about people all the time. Just start recording exactly what you observe. For example, it's Sunday and your son comes down bleary-eyed after breakfast is over. Do you notice the eagerness in his voice as he tells you about the super movie he saw last night, or do you observe that, once again, he has not made his bed and has come down without brushing his teeth?

You meet a stranger at an office party. Do you try to figure out his "importance" and the strength of his relationships with your boss, or do you notice the genuine twinkle in his eye and his obvious good nature? Do you notice that his shoes are scuffed or that he graciously compliments the waitress and makes her smile? Does your nose turn up because the table settings don't match, or do you acknowledge the effort your hostess is making to welcome you?

In short, with people and situations, do you focus on their weaknesses and what is "wrong," or do you appreciate their strengths and what is "right"? Most people, including you, do both. What is important is to find out in which direction you are tilting.

Now try this. Pick any person with whom you have an ongoing relationship and do not particularly like. It could be an in-law or a disagreeable coworker or a pompous parent in the PTA. Look for at least two traits in that person that you like and admire. Persist until you find them. Compliment that person on these traits and be sincere. If you cannot be sincere, don't do it.

Repeat this with other offensive people in your life.

See what happens to your life and your relationships with these individuals.

□

10

Why affirmations can actually hurt you and what to do about it

◨

THERE ARE MANY books out there that extol the virtues of affirmations. Most of them advise you to pick a problem that is troubling you and then craft an affirmation that addresses it. Have you just been fired and are perhaps terrified that you won't find another job? Affirm that you are the perfect candidate and many companies would be glad to avail themselves of your services. Or affirm that you are fully at peace and the perfect job will appear in your life at the perfect time. Are you concerned about your weight? Affirm that day by day the fat is melting away and you are reaching your ideal body mass index. Do financial worries keep you awake at night? Affirm that you have more than enough money to meet all your needs and add to your savings. Are you seeking a relationship? Affirm that the ideal person is in your life or will be shortly.

There is one problem with this approach. For far too many people, it doesn't work. Maybe you too have tried affirmations of various kinds and seen no result. You remain jobless and your unemployment compensation has run out, while your body mass index is now so poor that you no longer want to know what it is, you still can't sleep because all the bills have come due, and you continue to be desperately single. There is less and less conviction in your affirmations each day.

When you begin using affirmations with radiant hope and the results you expect do not transpire, you could well be knocked for a loop. It is not uncommon to slip into dejection or even depression. That is why I say that affirmations can actually be bad for you.

However, let me hasten to add that the problem does not lie in the affirmations. It lies in the way in which you use them. Most people try to use affirmations from a place of disbelief. This makes them a form of wishful thinking. For instance, you affirm that you are well off financially and are thinking, "But I can't even pay my bills, let alone go on vacation." Or you affirm that you are in a satisfying, nurturing relationship, and your actual mental chatter is, "Who am I kidding? I've been eating alone for months and will have another lonely dinner tonight."

Affirmations became popular due to the work of the French psychologist Émile Coué in the early twentieth century. Coué noticed that when he gave a potion to a patient and simultaneously praised its effectiveness, the results were significantly better than when he simply provided the medicine and said nothing. He was one of the first to discover and use the placebo effect, whereby people who thought they were being given a powerful medicine actually showed physiological improvement, even though the substance they had taken was clinically inert—like a sugar tablet.

Coué came to the conclusion that any idea that occupied your mind exclusively would turn into reality, and he developed a form of autosuggestion. He encouraged his patients to repeat to themselves, "Every day, in every way, I am getting better and better." He also came up with a routine in which they did so at specified times and in specified ways, and he achieved many remarkable cures.

What is not so well known is that Coué also discovered that his method would not work if the patient made an independent judgment about the affirmation, and he warned that, if used improperly, his method could be dangerous.

That is the nub. When you affirm something and feel deep down that you're kidding yourself, then you are. The mental chatter that spontaneously arises saying that what you're affirming is simply not true is a form of judgment, and it more than neutralizes the affirmation.

You have probably heard dynamic motivational speakers asserting that you can achieve anything you want and that all your limitations are self-imposed. It is true that your limitations are self-imposed, but this does not make them unreal. Oh no, they are very real indeed. That is why you have not had much luck with affirmations as a tool to get you out of the circumstances you find distasteful.

For affirmations to work as intended, two conditions are necessary:

- ⊡ At some level, you have to believe—*really* believe—that what you are affirming is possible, even likely.
- ⊡ You have to take appropriate action that matches what you are affirming.

The reason most people fail is that they choose an affirmation that is the exact opposite of the situation they are experiencing. Overweight people affirm that they are thin, financially struggling people affirm that they have abundant resources, desperately single people affirm that they are in a close relationship. They all wish it were so, but they *know* it is not.

Don't do this. Pick an affirmation that is closer to what you think is the truth. It doesn't matter what is possible or not. What matters is what *you* think is possible. Remember the scene in *Pretty Woman* where the prostitute played by Julia Roberts triumphantly reveals that she would have spent the night for half the sum paid, and the character played by Richard Gere amusedly divulges that he would have paid twice the sum he did. That's how it works. It is *your* belief that governs what you experience.

Having picked a suitable affirmation, you then have to act in accordance with it. If your desire is to lose weight, lay off the pizza and go to the gym. Affirmations can indeed manifest wonderful changes in your life, but you have to take actions that permit this to happen. You cannot expect to win the lottery if you don't buy a ticket.

◙

how to use affirmations effectively

Go back to any affirmation you've tried that didn't work. See if you can honestly believe that affirmation. If you can't, change it to one that seems within the realm of possibility. For example, you are in debt, and affirming that you're wealthy isn't working. Instead, try affirming that your level of debt is declining. Then act in accordance with your new affirmation. No more double lattes. Scissor your credit cards, and brown bag your lunch.

As each scaled-down affirmation comes to pass, you will gain the inner belief that is so crucial to making this game work. Do this regularly and you will soon be in a position to go back to the original affirmations you used. This time they *will* work.

◙

11

Not a trivial question

□

THINK OF YOUR life as it is right now. There is something you want quite a bit, possibly even desperately. A bigger house. A new car. A more congenial boss. A larger office. Better relations with your spouse. The ability to once more fit into the trousers—or dresses—at the back of your closet. A promotion so you can boss your irritating colleague around. Or maybe you want your in-laws to suddenly move to Australia. Your daughter to get into Princeton (and your neighbor's son to not get into any of the Ivy League schools). You want to become CEO. To become a media darling. To have paparazzi fighting to get exclusive pictures of you. Perhaps there's more than one thing you want; maybe there are two or three.

Now imagine that a genie—on temporary respite from serving Aladdin—gives you a choice. You can have the thing—or two things or three—you want, or you can get to the state where you have outgrown it.

Which would you choose? Why? Think well before you answer, because this is not a trivial question. It is really quite profound, and if and when you really come to grips with it, it can dramatically change your life.

Many decades ago, my family and I lived in Karol Bagh, a middle-class neighborhood in Delhi, and my parents took me to Janpath, an open shopping area with rows of vendors. There were also hawkers moving around with baskets of wares, and one of them had something that caught my eye. It was a brightly colored two-in-one children's book. One side, called *Just like Daddy*, was blue and featured a little boy who did various things like brushing his teeth and eating his breakfast "just like Daddy." The other side was pink and called *Just like Mommy*, and it followed a little girl who did various things just like her mother.

I really, really, really wanted that book and asked for it. It cost five rupees, a not-inconsiderable sum in those days for a family on one government bureaucrat income. My parents confabbed and voted no. The book had few pages and only about twenty words on each page. It did not count as literature, and I was already reading abridged versions of classics. For them, the decision was a no-brainer.

It did not sit well with me. I sulked. I withdrew emotionally from my parents in a marked manner and was chagrined when this withdrawal was not noticed. Like a skillful general, I changed tactics and bawled. The hawker kept pace with us, walking discreetly behind, and every time he caught my eye, he flashed the book. He had a touching faith in my ability to deliver. Perhaps dinner for his family hinged on my effort.

My mother was a frugal lady who, at the time, hardly ever bought anything for herself. She saw a purse she liked and was about to purchase it. It was my opening, and I grabbed it with the practiced ease of Tarzan reaching for the next vine. Raising a tearstained face, I howled louder and asked, between sobs, how she could possibly buy something so useless while denying me something so educational and useful. It was a low blow. It worked. Back went the purse. I got *Just like Daddy*. The hawker's children, I presume, got dinner. Dissension ruined what should have been a pleasant family outing. My parents withdrew from me in a marked manner, but I was too thrilled to care.

Some years ago, I came across the same book again, and the memories came flooding back. Once again, I experienced that insistent, uncontrollable desire. But it was a memory. I remembered clearly what I felt then, but I didn't feel it anymore. *Just like Daddy* now left me cold. I didn't want it. I didn't *not* want it. I didn't think about it, and it had no hold of any kind on me. I had simply outgrown my once-overpowering ardor for *Just like Daddy*.

You can readily think of similar examples in your own life. Can you recall a toy that you desperately desired that no longer has any hold on you? Or a former boyfriend about whom you were once passionate, and who now stirs no feelings at all?

So, would you rather get what you want? Or would you rather outgrow it?

———

Brij was the leader of a gang of brigands, dangerous and brutal. There was much blood on his hands and a price on his head, but so fearsome was his reputation that no one attempted to apprehend him. He had an extraordinarily vivid dream, one that kept repeating with startling clarity: He saw a holy man and somehow knew that the sage had something of great value. He knew that he had to get that thing.

One day, when Brij was walking alone in the jungle, he chanced across a traveler and instantly recognized the holy man of his dream. He promptly knocked the man down with his stave and dealt him a few blows to soften him up. "Give it to me! Give it to me now!" he screamed. "Where are you hiding the treasure?" In vain did the holy man protest that he had no treasure. The brigand searched his meager belongings. His bag had some food that was examined and thrown away. There were some stones and a few small silver ornaments, and the brigand pocketed the latter. They were not particularly valuable but offered some recompense for his effort. He searched diligently, even tearing the traveler's slippers and breaking his water pot. When he found nothing, he beat the holy man a few more times in frustration and walked away.

He had barely gone a dozen yards when he heard a feeble voice behind him calling him back. "Perhaps this is what you were looking for, my son," said the holy man, and he held up one of the stones the brigand had thrown away. Brij grabbed it, hit the man again for good measure, and departed.

A few months later, he was in a nearby town and, on a whim, visited the town jeweler and asked him to look at the stone. "Where did you get this?" asked the jeweler in astonishment. It was an uncut diamond of great value.

The jeweler offered him a princely sum, but Brij did not sell that stone. He borrowed against it and bribed the police and politicians to forget about his past. He set up a trading business and it flourished, making him a wealthy man. His caravans went to distant countries, bringing back exotic foods and unimagined luxuries. He married and begat children and became a prosperous citizen, with his days of crime far behind him. But his sleep was fitful, and there was something missing in his life.

A dream came again. He saw the same holy man and once more knew that the man had something of value that he had to get. The dream came with increasing frequency, and the former brigand knew that he would encounter the sage again.

Sure enough, the next week he came across the holy man making his way through the marketplace, leaning heavily on a stick. *Is it my doing that his leg is crooked*, the trader wondered guiltily.

Hurrying over, he greeted the holy man with great respect and begged him to visit his house. The sage agreed. Brij served him food with his own hands and fanned him while he rested. He observed that the holy man had no wrinkles, and his skin was as smooth as a baby's. There was ineffable peace on his face even when in repose. When the other woke and was ready to resume his journey, the trader fell at his feet and begged him to share the treasure.

"My son, you already took the treasure the last time we met," the holy man remarked, his eyes twinkling. "Do you not remember? I have nothing left."

With tears in his eyes, the ex-brigand repented his actions and begged for forgiveness. Rushing into his house, he returned with the stone he had preserved and held it out to the sage.

"This was the bauble I stole from you," sobbed the merchant. "Holy One, please accept this back and give me the real treasure you possess."

"What do you desire, my child?" queried the sage.

"Teach me," pleaded Brij. "Give me that which enabled you to give the stone away so freely. I now know that that is the real treasure you possess."

═

When you get what you want—what you have striven mightily for—there is a thrill of satisfaction. For a moment you are on a peak, and the vista is gorgeous. You feel like an emperor. This euphoria does not last. There is always another thing that you suddenly need. And another. And another. One by one, these longings take possession of you and flay you with whips as they goad you onto a treadmill that moves ever faster.

It is easy to outgrow a child's desire for a picture book. You don't have to do anything. The passage of a few years will do the trick. But can you really outgrow the things for which you now feel an insistent demand? Can you really shed the desires that have their claws in your mind and rend you apart? How can you do it? And will the void not be instantly replaced with a desire for still other things?

These are deep questions, and I will deal with them in the next few chapters.

回

what did you want ten years ago?

Go back ten years. Visualize the situation you were in as clearly as you can and what problems were troubling you then. What were the things you desperately wanted? Create as accurate a picture as you can of what your inner life was like then. Use your memory and refer to journals or diaries from that time if you have them. Talk to your parents, siblings, and friends and use their recollections as well.

How many of the problems resolved themselves? Odds are that most of the situations that kept you awake—the problems you thought were insurmountable—have simply gone away. They have disappeared like morning mist does when the sun comes out. How many of the things you wanted so desperately did you eventually obtain? Again, chances are that you did get many of them. Did it really matter? Did you get the lasting satisfaction you thought you would get?

Write down the lesson from this exercise. We will come back to it.

回

12

Are you *really* happy?
I suspect not

▣

DOES THE HAIR on your body stand up and do you sometimes tingle at the sheer joy of existing? As you go through the day, do you come radiantly alive with a deep sense of purpose? Are there many times when you feel like sinking to your knees in involuntary gratitude at the tremendous good fortune that has been bestowed on you? Do you sense, deep down, that you are doing exactly what you were put on earth to do, and is each day joyous beyond measure?

If your answer to most of these questions is no, can you clearly see that you are getting closer to it each week, each month, each year?

If your answer is again no, I humbly suggest that you are wasting your life. And life is far too short to be wasted.

Are you happy?

We tend to use the word *happy* cavalierly, and it has become debased. We are prone to say that trivial things make us "happy"—our favorite ice cream or chocolate, a promotion, going on a vacation, getting a day off from work, winning at bridge, our mother-in-law deciding not to drop by after all.

I am not talking about the momentary rush of good feeling you experience on such occasions. I am talking about a profound sense of well-being that is with you all the time. A deep knowledge that your life is on track and cannot deviate.

This does not mean that you do not face challenges, some of them quite serious. It does mean that even as you do what you must, you are still conscious that fundamentally you are fine and always will be. You cannot be anything else.

So, defined this way, are you happy? If not, why not?

The vast majority of people are not happy. Even those who seem to have it all—great career success, financial prosperity, a picture-perfect spouse and accomplished children, a sterling reputation—are not happy. They are not brimming with joy. Anxiety is a frequent and unwelcome guest in their lives. There is always an undercurrent of stress, and it overwhelms them all too often.

Many "successful" people (perhaps most of them) live in a world dominated by a giant to-do list, and it fills up relentlessly no matter how many items they scratch out. There is a constant feeling of low-level anxiety, a feeling that there is always too much to do and not enough time in which to do it. Henry David Thoreau was remarkably accurate when he observed that most people lead lives of quiet desperation and go to the grave with the "song" still with them.

Does this, perchance, describe your situation too? It doesn't have to! You *can* escape into the realm described at the beginning of this chapter and live there much of the time, if not always.

What do you have to get to be happy?

That is a good question. Say, as with Aladdin, a genie granted you three wishes. What would you ask for, and would it make you happy? Most people have a wish list featuring vast wealth, a trophy spouse, good health, close friends, a stimulating job, lots of leisure, and bright children, along with stuff like fame, power, and a body like Adonis or Aphrodite.

If you have such a list, throw it out. What I have to say may startle you.

There is nothing that you have to get, do, or be in order to be happy.

I repeat, *nothing*. In fact, happiness is your innate nature. It is hardwired into your being. It is part of your DNA. It is *always* with you.

The question that has probably popped into your mind is, "If happiness is my innate nature, how come I'm not experiencing it? How come I'm experiencing 'my life sucks'?"

My answer will startle you even more. You do not experience the happiness that is your innate nature because *you have spent your entire life learning to be unhappy.*

It is absolutely true, and you have done it unconsciously and unknowingly by accepting that you have to "get" something so you can "do" something so you can "be" something. Thus you feel that you have to get a lot of money so you can travel to exotic places so you can be happy. Or you have to have a relationship with a beautiful partner so you can have great sex so you can be happy.

These are all modifications of the if-then model, which says that *if* this happens, *then* you will be happy. I have heard thousands of variations on this. People say, "I would be happy if . . .

- ▣ I got a high-paying job.
- ▣ I became CEO.
- ▣ I married a beautiful and loving spouse.
- ▣ My son got into Harvard.
- ▣ My husband would show some interest in me and the house.
- ▣ My wife would stop nagging me the instant I turn on the game.
- ▣ I had children.
- ▣ My children would grow up and go to college.
- ▣ My in-laws moved to Australia.
- ▣ I lost twenty pounds.
- ▣ I didn't have this nagging headache all the time.
- ▣ I got ten million dollars.

And on and on and on.

Look at all the people around you and in your life. The only way in which you are different is the particular "if" you crave. Look back at your own life. You may have changed physically, but the principal difference between you now and you ten years ago is the particular items that appear on your if-then list.

This is really important, so don't rush on. Think of your life as it is right now, as you would describe it in your journal or to a close friend. It is an excellent idea to actually write your description down and read it again after a few days. You will notice that, explicitly or implicitly, you have a wish list in the document. *If* only this would happen, *then* you would be happy—or happier.

What you don't realize is that the if-then model is fundamentally flawed. The model itself is fallacious. But instead of recognizing this, you simply change the items on the "if" side of the equation.

A certain start-up entrepreneur dreamed of cracking a million dollars in annual revenue. Five years later, he was convinced that a hundred million was the mark that separates the men from the boys and something magical would happen when he crossed that line. He is now chasing a billion dollars and is not far from it.

Don't laugh. Variations of this are all around you and especially in your own life. Teenagers are ecstatic at the thought of getting their own set of wheels, and a beat-up, fifteen-year-old Dodge Dart is welcome. Two decades later, it takes a new Lexus to get the same feeling, and this one doesn't last either. What's next? A Ferrari? Or a Ferrari *and* a Rolls Royce? That won't do it either. Nor will a hundred-foot yacht or your own island off the coast of Greece.

Remember what I pointed out earlier. There is *nothing* that you have to get, do, or be in order to be happy. The pernicious effect of the if-then model is that it is supremely effective in preventing you from experiencing the happiness that is an inextricable part of you. The more you believe in that model and try to manipulate it to become happy, the more happiness eludes you.

That is how you learn to be unhappy, and most people never catch on to it.

▣

stuff does not make you happy

Think of the person you were ten years ago and what life was like then. Visualize it as clearly as you can. You had a wish list in those days as well. Re-create this list as accurately as possible. Chances are that many of the items on that long-ago list are now a regular part of your life. Has your sense of well-being increased?

Quite a few people are shocked to discover that it has not and wonder why. What about you?

▣

13

Happiness is your birthright—grab it now!

◙

MOST OF THE executives who attend my workshops are quite successful in conventional terms. Many have traveled widely, and they frequently tell me they've visited some deprived part of a developing country and were struck by the misery they observed. The people had nothing. "But they seemed so happy," the businesspeople note plaintively.

There is amazement in this observation and more than a hint of wistfulness. How can people who are so incredibly poor, so far removed from the "necessities" of modern life like electricity and indoor toilets and running water, still smile so genuinely? Why, with all of their good fortune, do the executives find it so difficult to beam happily at the world?

I asserted in Chapter 12 that happiness is inherent in you, that there is nothing you have to do to "get" it, that it is always with you and a part of your very nature. I also pointed out that you have spent a lifetime learning to be unhappy by buying into the if-then model and that this model is both beguiling and erroneous.

How do I know this, and more important, why should you believe me? You don't have to take my word for it. I will demonstrate the truth of it using your own life experience.

No matter how burdened you feel now or how troubled your past has been, you have experienced freedom in your life! Have you ever come across a scene of such spectacular beauty that it took you outside yourself into a place of profound serenity? A place of peace and healing calm? Perhaps it was a brilliant rainbow after a sharp shower. Or a snow-capped peak thrusting out of wispy clouds. Or the rolling ocean with big waves crashing in a hypnotic rhythm against pink sandstone cliffs. Or a jagged lightning flash in the midst of a storm of awesome, majestic power. Or an aurora twisting in the sky, changing color and shape continuously in a never-ending dance.

You can recall such an occasion. Virtually everyone can. Have you ever wondered why you experienced what you did? It was not the place or the scene. The travel industry grows rich off people who return to places of magical moments hoping to recapture them.

No! What happened was this: Somehow, inexplicably, at that instant, you accepted the world exactly as it was and you were OK with it. You didn't think, *That's a great rainbow, but it's off to one side. If I could move it two hundred yards to the right, it would be more symmetrical and look so much better.* Or, *That's a beautiful valley, but the tree in the foreground has too many crooked branches. If I had a chainsaw and twenty minutes, I could make it look really nice.*

Such thoughts never crossed your mind. The off-center rainbow was perfect in its skewed position. The crooked branches of the tree had their own charm and were, likewise, perfect in their gnarled presence.

When you accepted the scene exactly as it was, when you did not crave for it to be something else or different in some way, your habitual "wanting" self faded away. The happiness that is your inherent nature surfaced instantly, and you experienced its fullness. You didn't have to do anything. It rose of its own accord, and you felt it. You know you felt it, because you still remember this scene after all the years that have passed.

What you don't recognize, what you don't accept, is that your life is perfect.

That's right! Your life right now, with all of the trials and tribulations that you face, with all of the problems that weigh you down and cause you sleepless nights, is perfect. It is every bit as perfect as that scene you can recollect. And the only reason you do not experience that same well-being is that you don't believe this, you don't accept it. You are too busy rejecting one or more aspects of your life and striving with might and main to change it using the if-then model even though that model itself is flawed. No wonder you don't experience the joy, the sheer happiness that is your essential nature.

Does this mean that you should stop striving? That you shouldn't try to achieve goals? That you shouldn't try with all your might and main to improve your lot or build your business or accomplish great things?

Of course not! You should do all those things with every fiber of your being. But you need to do it from the knowledge that your success or failure has no bearing whatsoever on your essential well-being. If my entrepreneur friend from Chapter 12 achieves a billion dollars in sales, great—life is wonderful. If he does not, great—life is still wonderful.

The moment you sever that link in the if-then statement, the model drops dead. If "it" happens, fine. If it doesn't, still fine. You'll discover that life is a blast, every day is full of wondrous surprises, and all of life is a joyous journey of discovery.

Here is something strange, a wondrous paradox that many people have discovered. When you drop your insistence that something must happen in exactly the way you want it to, the chances of your getting what you desire increase greatly. That's just the way it is, and I describe why in Chapter 14.

Is it possible to sever the link in the if-then model? To accept life exactly as it presents itself, even while striving to achieve a vision? To live a life of great joy and fulfillment in which each day brings many moments of radiant aliveness?

Absolutely. It is a skill, no different from learning to ride a bicycle. The exercises in this book, if you do them diligently, will bring you to a high level of competence.

◙

to be happy, stop clinging

You are clinging, always clinging. Think about this seriously—how you are continually holding on to memories of the past. You have a great meal at a restaurant, instantly put it on your list of favorites, and go back to it. You like a book by an author and get her other books. You try a particular strategy at work and it is successful, so you repeat it over and over. Think about how you use memory all the time. You experience something as good or bad by comparing it with some event you have stored in your memory, something you cling to.

There is no question that this method simplifies life—perhaps this is the reason you do it. But when too much of your life is run by memory and you don't even know it, you lose the ability to experience life spontaneously. That's why the thrill of the rainbow or the verdant valley is so rare in your life.

Think about your life, every aspect of it. How much of what you do, experience, and think is governed by memories? (This will give you some idea of how constrained you really are.) Try to experience events without the burden of expectations dredged from your memories; then each moment will be liberating and exhilarating.

◙

14

Invest in the process,
not the outcome

◙

ALBERT EINSTEIN SUPPOSEDLY said that the definition
of insanity is doing the same thing over and over and
expecting different results.

Did you smile as you read this? Wipe it off your face! I'll
wager that, by this definition, you are a certifiable lunatic. You
too do a particular thing over and over. Sometimes you succeed; many more times you fail. Often you fail utterly. But
then you pick yourself up and do the same thing again and
again and again. Yet you expect different results, and when
you don't get them, you feel miserable and wonder why.

Don't feel too despondent, because you've had plenty of
help making this mistake and lots of company as well. This
particular mode of thinking and acting is a cultural norm. It
is extolled in elementary and high school, college, and the
workplace. There are training programs, books, and courses

that reaffirm it. Large numbers of people make the same error you do and are your buddies in misfortune.

What is this misstep that you and virtually everyone else make?

You invest heavily in the outcome. In fact, you invest exclusively in the outcome. A very dumb thing to do for reasons I will detail shortly.

First, a word of explanation. We are a goal-oriented society. From a young age, we are taught to set goals for ourselves and then work toward achieving them. Managers are encouraged to set stretch goals and then try hard to meet them. The focus is exclusively on the goal. If you achieve it, wonderful! You've succeeded. If you don't achieve it, terrible. You've failed. This starts early in life. You try to maintain a high grade point average, to get into a good—preferably Ivy League—college, to get a high-paying job with a prestigious company, to date an attractive person, to get promoted and rise in your company or succeed spectacularly in an entrepreneurial venture—to achieve, achieve, achieve.

Each of these "goals" is an outcome, and outcomes are totally beyond your control. Let me repeat that: *outcomes are totally beyond your control.* You can flawlessly execute the actions that you think will lead you to success and still not reach your desired outcome. Consider these examples:

——

Doug had been working long hours and traveling a lot. There were so many meetings that sometimes he couldn't even call his wife; sometimes he just forgot. It preyed on him, and he decided to make amends.

He visited the chicest store in the major European city he was in and—with the help of a salesgirl—selected an exquisite evening gown and had it gift wrapped. It was his way of expressing his love, and he looked forward to a weekend of intimate companionship when he got home.

His wife's lip curled when she saw what he had bought. "Don't you know I never wear stuff like that?" she began, and it went downhill from there. He slept on the living room sofa and was happy to escape to work on Monday.

Rosemary was a new manager and anxious to do things correctly, by the book. You couldn't arbitrarily fire a subordinate in the country where she worked—you had to "make a case" after warning him. So she kept meticulous records after she let her assistant know that his performance was unacceptable. He came in late from lunch, made personal phone calls on company time, and used only one side of the copier paper in violation of the company's conservation policies; she documented all this.

When she presented her findings to her boss, she expected a pat on the back for her diligence. Instead, he blew up. "Have you nothing better to do than keep tabs on how many minutes late he came back from lunch?" he stormed. She found herself warned instead.

Gary's company placed great emphasis on "teamwork" and "cooperation," and Gary was mindful of this. He curbed his naturally aggressive tendencies. When others accosted him, he bit his lip and replied politely. He went out of his way to do his share and more; he was so obliging that many of his coworkers commented favorably as they took advantage of his willingness to do what no one else wanted to. He thought he was a shoo-in for partnership, but he was passed over.

"You're a good worker," his manager assured him. "But you need more drive. You have to make tough decisions as a partner. Keep trying and you may make it in two years when the next batch of partners is selected."

———

Charlie hung up the phone, quivering with excitement. He had done it. He and he alone had accomplished this stunning feat. He was the executive vice president for development at a major state university and had just closed a deal with a wealthy entrepreneur: forty million dollars to put the benefactor's name on the business school! Now the school had the funds to hire top-notch faculty and start a Ph.D. program. "They have to make me president when the old codger retires next year," he thought disrespectfully of his boss. "They don't have other options anymore."

He organized a spectacular gala with a Nobel Prize laureate as guest speaker, along with celebrity entertainers. The businessman handed over the check and spoke about integrity and hard work, exhorting students to have the former and do the latter. It was a splendid success.

The very next week the entrepreneur was indicted on multiple counts of fraud and accused of bribing high public officials and of money laundering. It made the headlines of all the newspapers and the national evening news. Irate trustees accused Charlie of laxness in due diligence and forced his resignation. They, however, kept the money and "the old codger" wrangled himself a lusher pension.

———

Think back on your own life. Recall how many outcomes you have mightily worked for and failed to achieve. How bad did you feel after each failure? In all your life of striving, you have arrived at the outcomes you wanted only a tiny fraction of the time.

Remember, outcomes are outside your control. When you make your emotional well-being dependent on the achievement of a particular outcome, you are investing in that outcome. You are also setting yourself up for failure, dejection, and despair. Yet this is what you do time after time. You set yourself a goal—getting promoted, losing ten pounds, achieving a ten handicap at golf, learning Spanish—and then celebrate success or get dejected by failure. Even a cursory examination of your life will show that, more often than not, the outcome you wanted did not occur.

This practice is insanity, as described at the start of this chapter.

Is there a way out? Sure, there is. You can invest in the process rather than in the outcome, which is a learnable skill.

You do this by explicitly recognizing and acknowledging that outcomes are outside your command. You set your goal and determine your desired outcome, and having done that, you make your peace with whatever happens. If you succeed, wonderful! If you don't, still wonderful. Your happiness does *not* depend on whether or not you reach that outcome.

Actions are within your control, so you focus on what you have to do with every fiber of your being. You do it with full concentration and determination. In short, you invest in the process. The outcome, whatever it is, is fine with you. If you do get to where you wanted to, then wherever you get to becomes a new starting point, and you repeat the process all over again. And you do this time and time again.

When you function this way and invest in the process, you *cannot* fail. Every day becomes a blast. In fact, you won't be able to reach the vision I laid out in Chapter 12 if you don't master this method.

John Wooden was the first person to be inducted into the Basketball Hall of Fame as both a player and a coach. He led UCLA to an unprecedented ten NCAA titles during his last twelve years as a coach, and he knew all about investing in the process and not the outcome:

======

Many people are surprised to learn that in twenty-seven years at UCLA, I never once talked about winning. Instead, I would tell my players before the games, "When it's over, I want your head up. There's only one way for your head to be up, and that's for you, not me, to know that you gave the best effort of which you are capable. If you do that, then the score really doesn't matter, although I have a feeling that if you do that, the score will be to your liking." I honestly, deeply believe that in not stressing winning as such, we won more than we would have if we had stressed outscoring opponents.

======

The universe doesn't pay much attention to your puny wants. You can hang on grimly to your vision of how things should be, which is usually bruising and unpleasant. Or you can put your vision out there and strive for it, while embracing whatever comes your way—even as you keep trying to head in the general direction you have charted. This way is just plain fun and invigorating.

Learn to invest in the process, not the outcome.

▣

---

acceptance is the key

Pick any situation that is troubling you right now. Carefully describe it to yourself; it helps to actually write it down. See how all of the unease comes from your resistance to what is in front of you, from your staunch insistence that things have to be the way you want them to be.

This doesn't mean that you should give up all your plans and hopes. It does mean that you should strive as you always have but refuse to let an adverse outcome affect your equanimity.

Go back and read Chapter 4 once again. Learn to be a Daruma doll.

▣

15

On wild horses and freedom

▣

D O   Y O U   F E E L   life is more complex today than it was
three decades ago when there was no e-mail and no cell
phones, the Internet was used only by geeks, and fax machines
were leading-edge technology? I think so too.

Go back in time. Get a DVD of *Ben Hur*—the 1959 William Wyler classic—and watch it. If you don't have time to
view it all—this is a looooong film—watch Chapters 29 to 43.
There is a lesson for you—a very powerful lesson.

Ben Hur has escaped from being a galley slave and is
returning to Judea in style as the adopted son of Quintus
Arrius, consul of Rome. He meets Sheikh Ilderim, who has
raised exquisite, milky white horses. They are mettlesome
creatures, and time after time, they leave the track and crash
the chariot to which they are hitched. None of the drivers can
manage them. Sheikh Ilderim is adamant that whips and chas-
tising devices may not be used.

A few weeks later, these same horses sweep to victory in the climactic chariot race, triumphing over the black steeds of Roman tribune Messala, who freely uses his whip to no avail. Ben Hur has a keen eye for his horses' individual strengths and wins them over with affection.

You too preside over a charger that takes you into rough terrain and throws you off. It is a strapping creature that takes you on journeys you would rather not have taken, but there is nothing you can do about it.

I'm talking about your mind, that maelstrom of unruly emotions that resides between your ears and is constantly goading you to do something, then something else, and then something else that is different from the first two somethings. Tune in to the internal monologue you have going on in your head all the time:

＝＝

Hm, that's a good-looking girl—*really* good-looking. Wonder if she's married. No ring, but that doesn't mean anything these days. Maybe she has a boyfriend. I'd love to go out with her, but someone that beautiful probably has men in line, and the waiting list closed two years ago. Even if I did get a date with her, with my luck, I'd probably discover she's a lesbian. That's what happened with Amy. She married that investment banker. How could anyone marry such a twerp? He has buckteeth and he giggles—he actually *giggles*—and his face looks like a badly patched pothole. If ever Medusa saw him, she'd be the one to turn to stone. Wonder if he knows she's gay. She only married him because he's loaded. Still in his thirties and he already has a summer home and a winter home and a regular place in the city, and I bet his bonus was eight figures. With luck, she'll get it all in the divorce and then get hooked on cocaine. Serve them both right.

Why do women fall all over i-bankers? Scum of the earth. They stay awake at night figuring out new ways to rip off consumers, and when they get tired of that, they keep in practice by coming up with new ways to rip off the government. And the government raises my taxes to bail them out. Happens because all the politicos are on the make. Look at their contributor lists, full of morons from the financial service companies. That's what our so-called democracy has come to. It's just a marketplace, and if you have enough money, you can buy anything. They're all thieves, but some of them are bright, so they simply add zeroes to the amount they get away with. Maybe I should join them, since I sure as hell can't lick them. But who wants to get stuck in such a soul-deadening occupation? Even third-world garment workers have more interesting jobs. That's my problem; it's always been my problem. I want the money, but I don't want to be part of that stinking profession. Maybe it'd be worth it if I could get someone that gorgeous to go out with me.

She's getting up. She left her purse on the table. Now's my chance. I'll grab the bag and take it to her. Drat! She saw it was missing and came back. I could still go over and say hello. What if she snubbed me? What if I told her I was the casting director for the next Steven Spielberg film? Or should I simply be a scout for Ford or Wilhelmina or one of the big modeling agencies? What's the use? She's gone and I'll never see her again. I waited too long.

That's my second problem—I just don't take action. I have all these brilliant ideas, and then somehow I don't do anything about them. Why do I always procrastinate? I can have an hour to do a one-page report and all my preparation done, and I dawdle until I have ten minutes so I have to scramble and turn in stuff far below the standard I know I can produce. I think I must have a self-destructive impulse. Maybe its genetic. My father had the same thing, and I bet he passed it on to me. I can't fight DNA. Guess I'll just have to live with humdrum mediocrity.

═══

I bet you have some variation of this monologue going on in your head all the time. It *never* stops. Much of it is destructive because you run yourself down unmercifully. And it is totally out of control. Go back to *Ben Hur* and watch the footage of the chariots tumbling and crashing. That's exactly what's happening to you.

That restless, horrible, shrieking, gibbering monster that is your mind flays you continually and goads you into action—any action, anything to placate this agitated beast. Is it really as bad as this? It's actually worse. Am I exaggerating? No, I'm probably understating it.

Do you turn on the TV not because there is something you really want to watch but because you need to beguile your mind? Do you reach for the paper or a magazine or a book for the same reason? Do you browse the Internet randomly, clicking on links you have no real interest in? Do you feel uneasy if you simply sit down for a while with nothing to do and no intention of doing it anyway? Do you have a horrible feeling that time is slipping away and you haven't done as much as you should?

I conduct an exercise in which I have people sit quietly by themselves and do nothing. Very few last the recommended half hour. Many say they feel as if their head is ready to explode. Try this for yourself before you pass judgment. It is a simple task but by no means easy.

Here is a question for you to ponder: You like to think of yourself as a "free" person, and freedom is a virtue you probably prize highly. You define *freedom* as the absence of external restraints. How free are you really if you can't be with yourself for a half hour, if you can't sit quietly for a mere thirty minutes?

As the saying goes, the mind is a terrible master but a splendid servant. You want a well-trained steed that will take you where you want to go rather than to a random destination you have no desire to visit. A horse that will enable you to win the race.

I will show you how to begin training your monster in the next two chapters, but do the following exercise first.

▣

watch the movie of your mental chatter

Sit down in a comfortable chair. Put your feet up if you like, and relax your body. Now just watch your thoughts. Don't try to channel them, think of work-related stuff or problems you're having, or drift into a sexual fantasy. Just observe them as they flit in and out. See how many there are and how disjointed, how they arrive and dissipate and feed on each other. See how many times you run yourself down in some subtle fashion. See how often you are critical of others. Observe how strongly opinionated you are.

Think of this as an alternative to a visit to the movies. It is vastly more entertaining and costs a lot less. Even more important, this exercise is the first step to doing something that will profoundly change your life.

▣

16

Taming the horses—'tain't easy but it can be done

▣

L IKE MOST PEOPLE, you probably believe that you're agitated because of the way things are. You're upset because you have a toxic boss who constantly runs you down. You have financial worries because your income just isn't enough to meet your needs, your 401(K) has suffered in the market meltdown, the economy is bad so it isn't possible to get another job, and age is against you anyway. The problems are all outside. But are they really? Consider April's story.

═

It was still early when there was a loud knock on the door. Who could possibly be calling at this hour? April glanced out from the upstairs bedroom window. There were two men on the stoop outside. She could not see their faces because they wore regulation headgear. Both were in uniform.

Her heart sank. Some unseen hand seemed to have removed all the bones from her body and replaced them with sawdust. She couldn't move. She couldn't breathe. With a great effort, she pulled herself together and rushed downstairs, unmindful that she had lost one of her slippers. Her outstretched belly, bursting with the life that would shortly emerge, banged against the handrail, but she didn't heed it in her haste. She flung open the door and stood there panting. Worry lines creased her face as she looked at the men questioningly and asked them in.

They removed their caps as they entered and held them under their arms. Both men stood ramrod straight. They were not at attention, but they appeared to be. They looked at her sympathetically. "Is he . . . is he . . . ?" she stammered, unable to get the words out. Strange things were happening to her. She could feel her unborn child kicking. She was deathly cold and feverishly hot at the same time and in different parts of her body. Her infant daughter, awakened by the unusual noises, started bawling loudly.

The taller of the two men nodded. He too was deeply moved and seemed close to breaking down. "We're so sorry, ma'am," he choked, and then the tears came down. Still crying, he caught her expertly as she collapsed and laid her gently on the couch. The other man rushed to the kitchen to get a bowl of warm water and a towel. Gently he wiped her face and revived her.

For the next few days, April was in a haze, moving like an automaton. There seemed to be other people in the house—some familiar, some not. They helped her clean and bathe and feed her daughter. They made sure she ate at least something, sometime. She had no conscious memory of all this, just a vague understanding that they meant well. Time collapsed on itself and stretched on interminably.

Her husband was never going to come back. Ever. They weren't going to buy that tiny home in the new development they both loved. She would never again see him crinkle up his face and astonish visitors by touching the tip of his nose with his tongue. He'd practiced and practiced until he could do this and had been so proud. Her jaw had dropped in astonishment the first time she saw it, and he'd stood there grinning bashfully like a schoolboy.

The men in uniform came often and helped her around the house and talked to her. They belonged to the same unit, had served in the same theater of war, and had known her husband well. In some ways, they'd known him even better than she did. They told her how he would pass around pictures of her and her daughter and how those pictures got grimy from being in his shirt pocket over his heart, so he got himself some clear glue, cut strips of thick, transparent plastic, and laminated them. She burst out sobbing uncontrollably at this, and they were more circumspect from then on. Gradually they stopped coming.

Then one day, weeks later, they were back. The door was open, and they rushed in without knocking, whooping and hollering. Her husband was alive! The explosion had been massive, and then the enemy had attacked with mortars and rocket-propelled grenades. The bodies had been so badly burned that identification was difficult. Her husband had taken an early shot to the head and been knocked unconscious beneath a bush. It was a crease, and he eventually came to and found himself alone in enemy territory. He was weak from loss of blood and would have perished except that a peasant found him, hid him in his house, and nursed him back to health. Then, under cover of darkness, the man took him to the outskirts of his camp and pointed out the way.

A great joy seized April. He was alive! She would see him soon. She could talk to him right away. The soldiers were waiting to take her to the base, where she could speak to him in his hospital bed. The bits and tattered pieces of her dreams started reassembling themselves. She fainted, and in a reprise of their first visit, the tall soldier caught her and took her to the couch while the other went to the kitchen for water and a towel.

=====

Poignant tale, isn't it? Do you feel sorry for April, the pregnant, widowed mother of a young child who, as it turned out, was not a widow at all? Did you vicariously share her despair and exult with her reprieve? Quite a few people do. Empathy is a wonderful human emotion.

April's story has a really important lesson, one far deeper and more significant than sharing the suffering of a fellow human being. If you really learn this lesson, it will help you immeasurably in all kinds of situations. It will truly and completely turn your life around.

What is this momentous lesson? Simple. It is the knowledge that April made it all up! Nothing really happened. The anguish that gripped her? She manufactured it in her own mind, and it was strong enough to have a physical effect on her. The relief and joy she experienced? She created that herself too—in the same place. All on her own, all in her head, she went from pleasant existence to utter melancholy and then to exultant joy. She just never realized she was doing it.

You do this too. All the drama in your life—the hard times, the struggles, the misfortune, the lucky breaks—you make *all* of them up. They all exist in your head and only in your head.

This is where I get tremendous push back and vociferous protest from participants in my workshops. Some get really worked up. What do I mean she made it all up? Don't I know that the poor girl thought she had lost her husband and become the single mother of an infant with another on the way? What am I advocating, that she forget her husband immediately and move on? Don't I know what it means to be human? What kind of a monster am I?

I have heard it all. Before you jump on the accusatory bandwagon, pause for a moment, rein in your emotions, and consider what I'm really saying.

The emotions that April experienced were something she created in her mind. She thought they came from outside, but they really didn't. They were her conditioned reflex that came into play instantaneously. You too have gone through painful experiences and reacted in a similar fashion. You too originated all that turmoil in your mind and all by yourself.

Think of a continuum. At one end is someone who is completely bowled over by some tragic occurrence and unable to get on with life. Like the couple whose teenage son died in an accident. Twenty-five years later, they still keep his room exactly as it was on that day, speak in hushed tones about what he would have been like today, and mark occasions like the anniversary of the day he won an academic competition.

At the other end of the continuum is a trauma surgeon. Imagine a good one at work, especially in an inner-city hospital. She is completely focused on what she does as she gets patients with a wide variety of problems—gunshot wounds, stabbings, car accidents, heart attacks, poisonings, drug overdoses, and so on. She does what she has to do and then moves on. She struggles valiantly to save a desperately hurt patient, but if she fails and the patient dies, she simply moves on to the next case. She does not manufacture drama in her head. In fact, she would become ineffective and incompetent if she did. It bothers her to lose a patient, but she cannot stop to mourn because the next one needs her attention.

That is the continuum, and *you* get to decide where you want to be. You probably don't realize that you have a choice, but you do. And *that* is what I'm talking about.

Think about this seriously for a week before you even attempt to contradict me. Yes, I know that, unlike April in the story, you really have experienced terrible loss. Nevertheless, the misery you felt was something you created. You didn't have to create it. You probably didn't realize you were doing it. You were culturally conditioned to do so. But the net effect was the same—you sank into a welter of despondency when there was no need. Go back and read Chapter 2 again. It will make more sense to you now. See how incredibly generous you've been with the "bad thing" label.

What if the soldier in our story had actually been killed in that enemy attack? Would his wife's agony still have been made up? Indeed it would. It was so powerful precisely because we are socially and culturally conditioned to react this way. You don't have to travel that route. You can actually choose the path you want to traverse. You are still creating dramas in

your life. We will talk about how to stop this debilitating process in the next chapter.

▣

---

was it a tragedy? maybe not

Pick any incident in your life that you think of as a tragedy—
the death of a loved one, failure in a major undertaking, the
breakup of a serious relationship, a job loss, or financial rever-
sals. Recall the maelstrom of emotions that it created in you. If
the event happened some time ago, the turmoil will have sub-
sided, although thinking of it might stir it up again to some
extent. Think about the drama surrounding it; recognize and
acknowledge that you created that drama.

Take a deep breath and let the disquiet go.

▣

17

The Bard had it right!

□

IMAGINE THAT YOU'RE watching a horror movie, a really well-made one, in a theater. The acting is superb, the sound and special effects are terrific. It's a slasher flick, and various members of the cast come to grisly, untimely ends. You identify with the heroine as she searches for a way out. Her eyes are dilated, she swivels her head wildly, looking for the danger she knows is lurking close by. She moves toward the very spot she should avoid, and the tension becomes too much for you. Your heart is beating too fast, your mouth is parched, and your pulse is racing. All of a sudden you can't take it anymore.

What can you do? You can remind yourself that it's simply a stream of images flashing by at thirty frames per second on a curved white screen. Look at the exit signs off to the sides in dim red. See the person next to you with popcorn all over his shirtfront. Lean back in your seat and hear the springs squeak. The moment you do any of these things, you come out of the storyline and back into your normal and—I hope—less scary world.

What you have done is shift your focus, and that is enough to dispel the drama of the horror movie. What you don't realize is that you can do exactly the same thing in "real life," and the first step is to understand that you are always playing a role, but you are *not* the role.

William Shakespeare got it right when he had Jaques, the resident grump of the forest of Arden, point out,

All the world's a stage,
And all the men and women merely players;
They have their exits and their entrances,
And one man in his time plays many parts.

Jaques went on to define the parts in terms of the stages of life from infancy to old age, but the analogy holds for every role that you play.

Say you're an actor playing Willy Loman in a new screen production of *Death of a Salesman*. You really get into the role. You ache as your commissions decline and you no longer make the income you used to. You dream of bigger things but they do not materialize, and you suffer as you try to come to terms with it. You feel you are letting down your family and try your hand at suicide. You really go through agony.

But even as your character goes through this pain, you are riding on a high plane as an actor. Somewhere in the back of your mind is the thought that if Willy Loman is sufficiently realistic in his misery, then maybe, just maybe, there could be a Golden Globe nomination in your future, perhaps even an Academy Award. So you pull out all the stops and pour yourself into the role with gusto. Never was a salesman more disgruntled or disappointment written more clearly on his face. No one ever tried more desperately to end his life by inhaling gas or crashing cars.

All of this is bearable—not just bearable, but triumphantly bearable—because you know you're not Willy Loman. You're just a darn good actor playing the role of Willy Loman. Think about this again. This is hugely important. You're able to enjoy playing a deadbeat salesperson whose life is coming apart at the seams, because you know at a very deep level that you're not "him." You're playing him.

As the Bard of Avon put it so well, the world is a stage. What you're playing is a role. Whether CEO or fresh associate, president or intern, hooker or nun, takeover titan or unemployed automobile technician—they are all roles. Each of these roles comes with its own set of problems and constraints. Your task is to play that role with virtuoso abandon. And as long as you clearly recognize that you're playing that role, you're just fine.

Life becomes incredibly tough because you insist in identifying with the character and not the actor. You know that you can dispel the tension of a horror film by fixing your attention elsewhere. But you think there is nothing similar you can do about the manifold problems that beset you in "real life" because "this is not a movie."

That is a trap you fall into readily. You think you're stuck, that there is no escape. But you can set yourself free by recognizing that you're merely playing a role that you have identified with and shift your focus to who you really are.

So who are you if you're not your character? That's something we will cover in the next three chapters.

In the meantime, bear this in mind: If you identify with the actor, life is a ball. Every day is a thrilling adventure. If you identify with the character, you're screwed—or will be sooner or later.

▣

it's all impermanent, so why get bothered?

Here is *Ozymandias* by Percy Bysshe Shelley. He was speaking of Ramses II, the most powerful man in the world in the thirteenth century B.C. Think about its implications for you:

I met a traveler from an antique land
Who said: "Two vast and trunkless legs of stone
Stand in the desert. Near them on the sand,
Half sunk, a shattered visage lies, whose frown
And wrinkled lip and sneer of cold command
Tell that its sculptor well those passions read
Which yet survive, stamped on these lifeless things,
The hand that mocked them and the heart that fed.
And on the pedestal these words appear:
'My name is Ozymandias, King of Kings:
Look on my works, ye mighty, and despair!'

Nothing beside remains. Round the decay
Of that colossal wreck, boundless and bare,
The lone and level sands stretch far away."

Or ponder these words by Shakespeare:

Imperial Caesar dead and turned to clay
Might stop a hole to keep the wind away.
O, that that earth, which kept the world in awe
Should patch a wall t'expel the winter's flaw.

Recognize that, like Caesar, you inhabit this lump of clay.
You are not the lump of clay.

▣

18

The scientist who cheated.
You cheat too!

▣

How do you think of yourself, and how would you describe yourself to others? Would you say that you're logical and scientific? That you're not easily deceived? That you look at the facts before making a decision? Most people who attend my programs nod their heads at this. Yes, they are right-thinking people who look at the evidence—all of the evidence—before drawing conclusions. Of course, like you, they are honest individuals. At least, they think they are.

===

Dr. Al Newton was a distinguished physicist, perhaps the most illustrious ever, and certainly on the same level as the seventeenth-century Sir Isaac. Al had won every award, every honor. His insights into the world of matter were legendary. He advanced boundaries in particle physics (the world of the very small) and astronomy (the world of the unimaginably immense). That was why he was selected to become head of the jocularly named Ultimate Machine, which was the largest particle accelerator ever built at a cost greater than the gross domestic product of many countries. It would smash subatomic particles together at energies of 20 trillion electron volts and more in an attempt to re-create the conditions that existed in the seconds after the big bang gave birth to the universe.

Like its predecessor, the Large Hadron Collider, the Ultimate Machine did not quite reach its intended power, but it did succeed in achieving conditions that probably hadn't been seen since a microsecond after the big bang. Al had woven his experimental findings into a theoretical framework of incredible complexity to come up with a new "general model of everything." It was no big deal to weave electromagnetism and the strong and weak nuclear forces into a common structure, but Al was able to make a quantum leap and show how gravity could also be thrown into the mix. Precision data from the experiments he conducted seemed to back him up.

But there were credible and persistent rumors that Al had been fudging his data, and they became too numerous to ignore. Given the sensitivity of the matter and the eminence of the subject, the World Federation of Scientists chose to investigate it very quietly. Dr. Peggy Mandian, herself a celebrated physicist, was the lead investigator. Al was open and cooperative. He shared his experimental logs, his findings, and the calculations he made and took her through every step of the logical ladder he had constructed.

It all seemed to check out, except for one troubling matter. About 30 percent of his data did not fit into his model. Some of those data actually appeared to refute it. Peggy asked him about it.

"What are you referring to?" he asked, genuinely puzzled.

She showed him the data.

"Oh, that!" he exclaimed, his face clearing. "I just threw those out."

She was astounded at his open admission. "Why would you do that?" she gasped, unbelieving.

He seemed puzzled by her question. "Because those data aren't relevant," he replied.

She persisted, "Why were they not relevant?"

Al grew testy. "Because they're not real," he snapped.

"You did make these observations, did you not?" she pressed.

"Yes," he admitted grudgingly.

"Then why aren't they 'real'?" she inquired.

He exploded in a paroxysm of rage. He had much to say about idiotic bureaucratic investigators who had no clue about how research was done and how scientific theories were built and validated. He held forth at length on her intellectual limitations and got in some snide remarks about how her gender handicapped her.

Peggy gathered up her papers and left hurriedly.

She presented her findings in person to the board of the World Federation of Scientists. "I was taken aback at the intensity of his reaction," she told them. "But that was not what really blew my mind. What completely floored me was what happened later. I spoke to all of his team members individually. They were all candid and helpful. They were all stars in their field. They all admitted that they had ignored the data I drew to their attention. And none of them saw anything wrong in doing so. It seemed they genuinely could not comprehend my concern, and many grew angry when I persistently questioned them."

The board went into a conclave that lasted several hours. Then Peggy was summoned again. "We have studied your report carefully," the chairman began. "Very carefully indeed. Dr. Newton is a careful experimenter and the leading theorist of our time. None have come close to his lofty status. The theory he has proposed is paradigm busting. No one has ever propounded such a groundbreaking hypothesis and simultaneously backed it up with experimental data. What seems to be your concern?"

Peggy was flabbergasted. "But . . . but . . . he ignored almost a third of his observations," she finally got out. "He took no account of them at all."

"Of course he ignored them," the chairman agreed. "It was the right thing to do. They weren't real."

"I protest," Peggy began, but the chairman cut her off.

"Dr. Mandian, you are a well-regarded scientist and have achieved some renown," he said. His voice was gentle, but there was steel underneath it all the same. "I have directed your report to be withdrawn and sealed. I would recommend that you take a long vacation and then resume your research. You have been working hard—a sabbatical is in order, and I will arrange one for you—at full pay, of course."

He looked at her inquiringly, and his expression told her that she had better accept gracefully. She did.

Am I crazy? Or is everyone else? was the thought that kept badgering her for the rest of her life.

⸻

What was your reaction to the tale of a scientist who ignored a good chunk of his data and used only what fit his design? Should Peggy have persisted? What would you have done? And why was everyone so ready to side with Al? Was it a wide-ranging conspiracy? Do such conspiracies really exist?

What if I were to suggest that you too are guilty of the same high crimes and misdemeanors? That you also ignore information that does not fit your model? That everyone around you does the same, and you all encourage each other in this collective, willful blindness?

Well, you do!

Not convinced? Let's begin with how you describe yourself. Here is an account by John, a participant in one of my workshops. It is likely similar to what you might say:

Hi, I'm John, and I'm a software engineer. I work for a start-up that built a better Web browser and is trying to get it accepted, but not enough people are using it, and we're running out of money. I'm forty-two, and age is against me, so I'm a little worried about what I'll do if the company folds.

I'm married to Amy, who is the COO—which means head honcho, since her company doesn't use the CEO title—at a nonprofit that runs programs for inner-city kids who have been deemed to be "at risk." We have two lovely children, a Labrador, and a golden retriever.

To tell the truth, Amy and I don't get along all that well nowadays, and there are times when I dream of pulling the plug. If it weren't for the kids, I'd have walked out long ago. Amy is a swell woman, but she nags too much and won't leave me alone. She's always after me to do something or other and make more money. That seems to be a bee in her bonnet. She keeps talking about the neurosurgeon who wanted to marry her. I wish he had—would have been a lot easier for me.

Still, it could have been a lot worse. I do like her, kind of, and she kind of likes me. Not like some of the couples in our bridge club, who battle viciously all the time. Her parents have never accepted me—they think she married beneath her—whereas my parents really embraced her. I wonder how my folks would react if they knew what I was thinking.

═══

John is convinced that he has accurately described his life. That what he has put down is the reality. You would probably describe your life in a similar fashion and are equally convinced about its reality.

Now consider this: Every day, for countless hours, John is not a programmer working for a tottering company while deciding what to do about a faltering marriage. Instead, he is an emperor who battles hordes and emerges victorious, a top tennis player who effortlessly vanquishes opponents on the way to a grand slam trophy, or a hapless victim being chased down a dark alley by a sadistic killer. Or he simply disappears—there is no John, no Amy, and no children. Certainly no parents who are accepting or unaccepting of spouses.

Puzzled?

It happens when he goes to bed and starts dreaming. His persona disappears entirely when he drifts off into deep sleep.

I can see your face clear. "Ah!" you exclaim. "But that's only a dream. It's not real."

I rest my case. You are no different than Dr. Al Newton.

If you're John, with a self-description that matches his, then somewhere between a quarter and a third of the time you (John) are not a software engineer. You have no spouse or children and are actually a variety of individuals undergoing bewilderingly different experiences. Some of the time you vanish. Poof! Just like that. Now that I explicitly point it out to you, you agree. Yes, this is exactly how it is.

But when you describe your life, you persist in being John the software engineer with a shaky job and an unstable marriage. What about all the other stuff? You throw it away. You don't even consider mentioning it. It's just a dream; it doesn't exist. It's *not real*!

If John the software engineer is who you really are, then you would be that person *all* the time. But you're not. And if you're not him some of the time, is it just possible that you're not him at all? That you're really somebody or something else?

A good model should explain all observations. Your model of who you are doesn't. You're ignoring a big chunk of your experience, and everyone around you is doing the same and egging you on. Is this or is this not crazy?

Remember what I said in Chapter 17? If you identify with the actor, you're fine. In fact, you're golden. If you identify with the character, you're sunk.

John, the software engineer, is also a character. He comes and goes, and his persistence is illusory. Perhaps you're beginning to glimpse this now.

Then who are you really?

We will cover this in the next two chapters.

▣

be the witness of the drama

Imagine that you are the great Director in the Sky, the orchestrator of all events in the movie of your life. You are a meticulous worker; every detail in your character's life has been planned. But now you're not the character. Observe your life as someone else who is intimately familiar with every aspect of your situation—your thoughts, your feelings, your hopes and aspirations—might view it. See the drama and pathos as if you were the audience of a staged play.

This is not easy to do, and you probably won't succeed in your first attempt. Keep trying until you succeed. You will if you keep trying.

▣

19

A *hugely* important question: who am I?

□

Y OU'RE AT A party and are introduced to someone you find extremely attractive who asks about you. What do you say?

A senior executive is interviewing you for what you're sure is your dream job and asks you to talk about yourself. What do you say?

You're ready to buy a co-op in Manhattan and have found one you like. Your financing is ready, and the only thing you're waiting for is approval by the co-op board. You're called for an interview and asked about yourself. What do you say?

Think about the myriad occasions that require you to describe yourself and what you say each time. Sometimes you put on a front, and sometimes you tell the truth. In your own mind, you're clear about when you're doing which. But the odds are good that you haven't given much conscious thought to the question of who you are. I'm suggesting that every time you begin a sentence with "I am . . ." and add something, anything, to the statement, you're being superficial and not quite accurate.

I will readily grant that you don't intend to be dishonest. You're more likely like Arthur Simpson—Peter Ustinov's Oscar-winning role in the movie *Topkapi*—who was unaware that the car he was driving to Istanbul was loaded with illegal arms. But, as in his case, the ignorance still costs you.

Let's start with the proposition that who you really are is something that is true *all* the time, something that can never be taken from you. That whatever your description is, it should be universally true and incorporate all your observations. You don't want to do an Al Newton (see Chapter 18) and ignore any data!

Bear with me as I postulate some horrible scenarios and try to ram home the idea that the model(s) you use to describe yourself are faulty and/or incomplete.

Do you describe yourself as John, the software engineer? That can easily be altered. You can change your name and become Joe. You can go to school and learn a new trade or just decide to become a beach bum. If you then describe yourself as Joe the beach bum, that too can change.

Do you define yourself in terms of relationships—X's child, Y's spouse, Z's parent, and so on? What if X, Y, and Z all perish in a calamity? Do you still identify yourself with those relationships by tacking the word *former* onto the descriptions? In any case, all relationships vanish when you're dreaming or in deep sleep. They disappear completely, no matter how strong they are in your waking state.

How about your body? This is a major locus of identification. Who you are ends at the tip of your nose—or the curve of your midriff. A bullet passes between the fingers of your hand, and you say you're delighted because it missed "me."

What if I were to take a machete and chop off your arm at the shoulder in a messy enough fashion that even the most skilled microsurgeon couldn't sew it back on. After you recovered, what of the severed limb, now shriveled and lifeless? Would it still be yours? If it were cut or burnt, would you still feel that "I" was hurt?

What if you were afflicted by a degenerative nerve disease that left you "locked in"—a condition in which you have no means at all of communicating with the outside world? No vocal chords, no gestures, no eye-blinking to painfully spell out words? Would you still identify with your body?

Do you identify with emotions—anger, fear, hate, jealousy, joy? All these come and go, as you well know.

What about your thoughts? René Descartes famously and incorrectly proclaimed, "I think, therefore I am." Thought arises in you because you exist, so he got it precisely backward. Let's go deeper. Whatever you can observe is not you, and I invite you to observe your thoughts. You're not used to doing this, but with a little bit of practice, you can do so easily. You observe yourself thinking and being angry, roiling with emotions. So that's not who you are.

Whatever you add to the statement "I am . . ." can be refuted. The descriptor can change. It disappears in the dream and deep sleep states. It's not something that is immutably and forever you. Try all the various ways in which you are prone to describe yourself. Each of them is valid, but only partially and only in a particular set of circumstances.

You play many roles—child, parent, lover, friend, employee, concerned citizen—and each of these is who you are, but none of them is who you are *all* the time. You slip into and out of these roles with the ease of a chameleon changing color.

Think about this. Who are you really? Who are you *all* the time? What is it that never goes away, that can never be refuted? What is it that persists right through your dream, deep sleep, and waking states?

Give up? The answer is simple, and you'll recognize it readily when I tell you. The only thing that never goes away is your awareness, the observer that knows you exist. "*I am*" is the constant. Not "I am . . ." followed by a qualifier.

That consciousness that you exist is with you like the screen that underlies all the movies that play in a theater. It never goes away. It's there in the waking state and in the dream state, and it's what lets you know that you slept well—or didn't—when you awaken.

You are that consciousness.

Why didn't this occur to you? Because you're always surrounded by it and never away from it; it has always been and will always be who you are. So you are not conscious of it, just like you're not conscious of the air you breathe, and the fish is unaware of the water in which it swims.

What is consciousness, and what can you do to identify with it and not the transient roles that you assume? We'll cover that in Chapter 20.

◙

don't hold on—it's *all* transient

Here is an old Sufi tale with a powerful message. The only way you'll be able to access that message is if you let the story seep into your being, your very consciousness, and grapple with its implications for you in every aspect of your life. It won't have much impact if you read it merely as an instructive story:

===

He was a holy man, and his eyes were so bright with transcendent knowledge that none of the guards dared stop him or lay a hand on him. He made his way to the durbar room of the sultan's palace and pounded the floor with his staff. "Who is the owner of this caravansary (inn)?" he demanded. "Bring him here at once."

Various ministers came and then the vizier, but the holy man impatiently shooed them off. Again he demanded to see the owner.

At length, intrigued by the strangeness of the event, the sultan himself appeared in his royal robes.

"Are you the owner of this caravansary?" the old man queried. "I seek shelter for the night and will leave in the morning."

"Gladly will my men provide for you this night," said the sultan amusedly. "But know that you have entered the royal palace. This is no caravansary."

The sage squinted. He came closer and peered at the sultan's face. "I recognize you," he exclaimed. "I was here three decades ago, and you gave me accommodation then."

"That was my father," said the sultan. "He is no more. May his soul rest in peace."

"I came two decades before that also," remembered the mystic, "and sojourned for the night. Was it then your father who made me welcome?"

"That was my grandfather," replied the sultan. "My father assumed the throne when his father crossed the great divide."

"And this place where people tarry for a while and then leave," thundered the seer. "Do you still say it is not a caravansary?"

——

20

Another hugely important question

□

S O YOU'RE NOT who you think you are in terms of what you do, who you're related to, or any of the other normal answers you give when asked about yourself. You are consciousness. But what does that mean, and how can you make any practical use of this knowledge?

This is where we start going deeper down the rabbit hole. This chapter gives you a different model of who you are and what the world is all about. You probably have not spent much—or any—time thinking about this. It's also possible that you will find yourself instantly rejecting what is presented here in a knee-jerk reaction. Certainly you will feel uneasy about accepting it. Recognize that the rejection doesn't come from you—it's simply a manifestation of the conditioning that you have been subject to for decades.

Recognize also that your intellect is a powerful tool, and you have made good use of it. But if you seek answers to the deeper questions—Who am I? What am I doing here? Where am I going?—your intellect won't be able to give them to you. Think of your intellect as a powerful sports car. You want to visit your friend on the other side of town. The sports car will get you to his house, perhaps even into his driveway, but then you have to leave it to enter the house and meet your friend.

In similar fashion, I'll use logic to satisfy your intellect for much of this journey we're about to begin. But it will only change your life if, after you get to a certain point, you can drop your thinking, calculating, analytical mind and step into the unknown.

The Indian sage Ramana Maharshi described it this way: "When the fire is not burning well, you pick up a stick from it and stir the fire. That gets the blaze going. When the flames start dying, then you throw in the stick you picked up and that gets burnt as well." The stick you picked up is your intellect. It too has to go if you are to reach the final destination of knowledge.

Let's start with Aristotelian philosophy and the acceptance that for every object there is an efficient cause and a material cause. The *efficient cause* is the agent that brings something about. Thus, if the object you're considering is a statue, the efficient cause is the sculptor. If you contemplate a gold necklace, the efficient cause is the goldsmith.

The *material cause* is the substance of which something is composed. For the statue, it might be marble or stone or bronze, and for the necklace, it's gold. This holds for all things. If you pick an automobile, the efficient cause may be General Motors and the material cause is steel, rubber, glass, and so on.

Now here is where it starts getting interesting. Every material cause also has an efficient cause. So the answer to the question "Who made the necklace?" is the goldsmith. The answer to "What did he make the necklace out of?" is gold. But then we run into "Who made the gold?" and "What did he make that out of?"

It's readily obvious that there is a whole chain of players behind the simple act of getting the gold into the hands of the goldsmith so he can fashion the necklace. There are mining companies, refining processes, manufacturers of chemicals, and so on.

Now let's apply this on a grand scale to an impossibly mammoth entity—the observable universe with its planets, solar systems, galaxies, black holes, and all the rest. The first question is "Who made the universe?" and the answer—from theology—is God. We follow up with "What did God make the universe out of?" Here we run into the limits of logic. A present-day physicist's response would be that God made the universe out of some quantum soup that includes elementary particles like quarks, leptons, and gauge bosons.

Let's press on. Who made the quantum soup, and what was the material cause of that? It quickly becomes obvious that we are now in a state of infinite regress. No matter what we postulate as the material cause, we get stumped by the "Who made it?" question.

Spend five minutes really thinking about this. It's simply a refined, more complex version of the "Which came first, the chicken or the egg?" question.

Now we come to the part that will really blow your mind. At least, it will if you truly open yourself up to all of the ramifications of the postulate I'm about to share with you.

The only way out of this infinite regression is to accept that "God" made the universe out of himself/herself/itself. There is the ultimate efficient cause that we arbitrarily call God and he/she/it made the universe out of God-stuff!

So *everything* around you is God-stuff. You, me, the book you're reading, the chair on which you're sitting, the dog turd on the road, the milk in your refrigerator—all God-stuff. The evildoers of history—Hitler, Stalin, Ivan the Terrible, Pol Pot—and the great figures of history—Lincoln, Gandhi, Buddha, Joan of Arc—all God-stuff.

There has never been, there is not now, nor will there ever be anything in the universe that is not God-stuff. The tyrant who's your boss, the enormously attractive date you're trying to ensnare—all God-stuff. And you, don't forget you—also God-stuff.

Recognizing this commonality beneath the surface is the great unity that mystics proclaim. Can you anchor yourself in this knowledge that you're not a-rag-and-a-bone-and-a-hank-of-hair but are descended from and no different than the creator of all that is?

Many spiritual masters proclaim that you can. They assert that this deep realization is, in fact, the purpose of life itself.

But it's neither easy nor certain and could take many lifetimes to attain. No matter. Here's how you can profit.

You may or may not experience the great unity of which you are a part in this model, but even an open-minded attempt to come to terms with it will make it much easier for you to identify with the actor and not the role. And that, as we've already discussed, will take you a great distance toward the ideal life vision laid out in Chapter 7.

回

the ultimate philosophical conundrum

The logical mind is a great asset, but it's also a barrier to higher understanding. Many stratagems have been developed to show you how to transcend your mind and reach such awareness. Zen koans are so absurd on first reading—"Imagine the sound of one hand clapping," "What was your face like before you were born?" or "What is the color of the wind?"—that grappling with them intensely can take you to a whole new level of consciousness.

Here is a question for you to ponder, one that many people consider the most important question of all and the root of all unhappiness and bondage: "How did the One become Many?"

回

21

There are no mechanisms!

□

WE'VE COVERED A lot of ground in the last few chapters, so a pause to decompress and take it a little easy for a while is an excellent idea. In this and the next several chapters, let's talk about the implications and practical uses of the ideas I've put before you.

How do you relate to other people? Take note of your chattering monkey mind and see how calculating it is. See how you view other people as mechanisms for achieving what you want. This worldview is deeply ingrained in every aspect of our culture. Do you have people reporting to you at work? You have to "manage" them well so they'll perform at high levels. When they do perform well, they reach organizational goals that show you in a good light. You get promoted or given more responsibility or better pay or some combination of the three. This forms the background and gives context to all your interactions with your subordinates.

Do you hang out with friends? See how you place a heavy burden on them—the burden of meeting your expectations and making you feel good. They have to call you and spend time with you and make you feel good and cater to your many whims. If they don't, you feel let down.

Step back a moment and see how you view everything and everybody through the prism of how they fulfill your wants and needs. The problem in doing this is that others become mechanisms that you use to obtain something you want. You tend to view the world as being put there for your gratification, and you take what you can when you can. Whatever prevents you from doing this is viewed as an obstacle to be overcome.

To get what you want, you start to divide up the universe into "us" and "them." In the "us" group are people you identify with in some way, people who are well disposed to you and whom you can trust. For most people, this would include family and friends and members of certain groups to which they belong. "Them" is everybody else.

You spend all your time looking after "me" and then "us" and really aren't very concerned about "them." Taken to an extreme, it becomes OK to bomb and kill "them"—that's what wars are all about.

Ram Dass—the author of *Be Here Now* and a former Harvard professor—relates an interesting anecdote in his book *Paths to God.* He had just issued a six-record program called *Love Serve Remember,* and it was selling briskly:

My father said to me, "I saw those records you put out. They look great. But I can't understand: Why are you selling them so cheaply? You're selling six records for four and a half dollars? You could probably get fifteen dollars for those records—well, nine, anyway!"

I said, "Yeah, Dad, I know, but it only costs us four and a half dollars to produce them."

He asked, "How many have you sold?"

I said, "About ten thousand."

He said, "Would those same people have paid nine dollars?"

I said, "Yeah, probably they would have paid nine."

"You could have charged nine and you only charged four-fifty? What are you, against capitalism or something?"

I tried to think how I could explain it to him. My father was a lawyer, so I said, "Dad, didn't you just try a case for Uncle Henry?"

He said, "Yeah."

I asked, "Was it a tough case?"

He said, "Oh, you bet. Very tough."

"Did you win it?"

"Yeah," he said, "but I'll tell you, I had to spend a lot of time on that damn case. I was at the law library every night, I had to talk to the judge—a very difficult case."

I said, "Boy, I'll bet you charged him an arm and a leg for that one!" (My father used to charge pretty hefty fees.)

My father looked at me as if I'd gone crazy. He said, "What! Are you out of your mind? Of course I didn't charge him—Uncle Henry is family."

I said, "Well, Dad, that's my predicament. If you show me any-body who isn't Uncle Henry, I'll happily rip him off."

—————

Now here is something for you to consider: The smaller the circle of people you think of as "us," the more difficult your life will be and the more problematic your relations. The larger your circle of inclusion, the more support you'll receive—no matter what the nature of the problem you're grappling with.

Chapter 20 gave you a model that emphasizes the underlying unity of everything and everybody. It's all God-stuff anyway, no matter how it appears. If you focus on that and try, however imperfectly, to bear it in mind, you'll find yourself becoming much more tolerant and better able to see the world as others do, thus making "allowance for their doubting too" (as Rudyard Kipling said so elegantly). Your attitude will communicate itself to others and make them more accommodating to you as well. It starts a virtuous upward spiral, and that is precisely what you want.

□

step outside your me-centered worldview

When you think of people, do you notice the similarities—same interests, similar background, common political views, coinciding economic perspective—or the differences—sex, age, gender, race, religion?

There is one way in which every single person is similar to you. Everyone is desperately seeking happiness. Everyone is thinking, "I want happiness. May I find it now and ever more. May I never suffer."

You want happiness and don't want sorrow; it's the same with everyone else. But your normal reaction is to examine how others can assist you in your quest. If you're conscious that everyone has the same desire, then you find yourself gravitating toward being of service instead of being demanding.

Pick a person each day, and on some days, choose someone you don't particularly care for. See if you can expand your circle of acceptance to include that person. How can you be of service to that person in the common quest of all human beings? Do it as sincerely as you can and observe what it does to your emotional state.

Other people are not put on this earth to be mechanisms for you to achieve your ends. Think about this until it really sinks in.

▣

22

How big is your pile?

◙

A FEW YEARS AGO, a leading financial newspaper ran an article on the "Masters of the Universe" and those primed to reach membership in that club. For the most part, they were high executives at financial service companies, and many ran hedge funds or private equity firms. The article noted that for the eager young men and women—mostly men—dreaming of joining the group, a mammoth increase in remuneration actually made them feel poor and deprived. The article noted that when these up-and-coming titans went from annual incomes of $250K to $750K, their financial insecurity increased manyfold.

The reason for this was also noted. At their new income level, they started rubbing shoulders with the very well heeled, the plutocrats whose wealth largely insulates them from having anything to do with the hoi polloi—also known as ordinary citizens. The newcomers were able to buy some of the toys of the ultrarich, but not all. The chauffeured limousines they already had, but they couldn't afford the private jets or the helicopter to whisk them over the snarled traffic to summer homes in the Hamptons. They had the apartment in the city, but not one with two formal drawing rooms and separate maid quarters. And they wanted all of this so much that they went into hock to get it. As high as their income was by conventional standards, they wound up enduring as much financial stress as they had when they took big loans to pay for business school.

These were not dummies. They had elite educations and had survived grueling rounds of screening at various colleges and prestigious companies. Their IQs were certainly much above average, and they were better informed than most. In calmer moments, if you could get them away from the hurly-burly, they would have joined you in laughing at the notion that anyone making the kind of money they did could feel deprived. But that is precisely how they felt when members of the group they aspired to join surrounded them.

Don't cluck your tongue in sympathy or sorrow. You too are stuck on the same flypaper—just a different part of it. Go back and read Chapter 13 again. See how firmly you are wedded to the if-then model and how everyone else around you is also.

Our entire economic system is based on the notion that things will bring you happiness. The mammoth advertising industry is constantly bombarding—and beguiling—you with pictures of stuff, all kinds of stuff, and linking them to images of desired emotional states, imprinting you with the idea that consumption is the way to reach such states. Beer commercials depict friends reveling in each other's company. Cosmetic advertisements show newly glamorous women capturing handsome men. Thirty-second travel industry creations show handsome, loving couples relaxing in exotic locations. They don't explicitly say, "If you buy this, you'll feel like that," but they don't have to. The powerful imagery they create says it better than words ever could.

=

Justin was just a kid, and his mom and dad had been fighting all the time. Then one day his dad wasn't there anymore. He didn't understand why and burst out crying at odd intervals, so his mom took him a long distance away to what she called a "working farm." He was thrilled. There were four-footed creatures there that he'd never seen before. Some were called cows, and they were common; some were called buffalo, and they were apparently quite rare.

The farmer's son Greg was his own age, and they played together all day and had a ball. One day they played a game in which they collected all of the pasty yellow stuff that dotted the field to see who could get the most in the shortest time. Justin raced all over, but Greg was quicker and got more of it. And then—how marvelous!—Justin discovered big mounds of it right behind the salt lick that all the animals spent time at.

Hurriedly he took off his T-shirt, scooped up as much of it as he could, and rushed back to add to his pile. It was on his third trip that his mother came out and let out a horrified scream. Grabbing him by the ear, she took Justin to the hand pump and made him strip right there. She then poured buckets of water over him and marched him straight to the bathroom and into the shower. She didn't leave him by himself as she had just begun doing; she held him and scrubbed him raw, scolding him all the time.

"Don't you ever play with s**t, again," she screamed.

"My pile of s**t was bigger than his pile of s**t," Justin said sullenly, not understanding what all the fuss was about.

===

Did you grimace uncomfortably as you read this story? Did it hit too close to home, and are you, at some level, rebelling against the comparison?

There are times in all of our lives when we see with crystal clarity that we are stuck on a treadmill that's going nowhere. One common occasion is when we're confronted with the death of a beloved relative or close friend. Think of the last time this happened to you. Do you recall the poignancy of the occasion? How quickly you understood the insignificance of whatever else was bothering you at the time? How suddenly your incessant quest for more stuff was revealed as a futile waste of time?

In India, there is a term for such realization. It can be loosely translated as the "dispassion of the cremation ground." It is profound. It is also short-lived. It doesn't take long for the understanding to dim and for you to get back on the merry-go-round.

Am I saying that whatever you're engaged in is a waste of time? Not at all. What I am saying is that linking your emotional well-being to the outcome of what you're striving for is a flawed strategy. You heard this before when I urged you to invest in the process, not the outcome. You now have another tool. Think of the underlying unity of all people and strive to be of service. Don't "gather ye rosebuds while ye may" with desperate urgency. Pause to strew some of those rosebuds around.

▣

what your old, wise self can tell you

This exercise is a common one in many traditions and is a favorite of Marshall Goldsmith, a leading executive coach.

Imagine that you're very old and about to hand in your dinner pail. Your body is worn out and has become a burden. You're happy to let it go. You're given one great gift—the ability to leave your final mark on the world. In front of you, eager to hear your words, is the person you are today. You see very clearly all of the trials and tribulations this person is facing, and you accurately see the probable outcomes of the actions your younger self is contemplating.

What advice would you give this younger self?

Write it down, and starting right now, follow that advice!

▣

23

Where are they now?

◙

MANY PARENTS OF a certain age will relate readily to the following tale. Some years ago, I got up at 4:00 A.M. and left the house fifteen minutes later. I went to a department store close by and stood outside the door. I thought I would be first in line, but I was mistaken. I wasn't even in the first hundred. We all waited in the predawn darkness, stamping our feet to keep warm.

It was rumored—always rumors, there was no hard information—that the store had gotten a new consignment of Cabbage Patch Kids and would be releasing them at 8:00 A.M. sharp. I had been delegated to make sure I got one for my daughter. Not just any Cabbage Patch Kid, mind you—because my daughter already had several—but a particular one. I don't remember the doll's name anymore, but I do remember how urgently I was charged with the task of capturing her. I looked with distaste at the swirling mass of humanity around me. They were the enemy, and I was girding for battle. I had to win. If I didn't, there would be wailing; it was clearly understood that I would have failed as a father and failed big. I think I flunked that test, but I'm not sure.

Then there were the Tamagotchis. These electronic kids needed lots of attention. They had to be fed at regular intervals and burped afterward. They had to be exercised and have their diapers changed. Kids were spending so much time "caring" for their Tamagotchis that it disrupted classroom lectures, and they were banned from my children's school. So the parents got to care for the Tamagotchis while the kids were in school. I was a marketing professor in those days and remember trying frantically to figure out why my daughter's Tamagotchi was sick and about to die. Fortunately, one of my students was hip enough to take a look at it for me, and after she ministered to it for a few minutes, the Tamagotchi was blooming with health. It died by my hand a few days later because I forgot to change its diaper, and I was in the doghouse for a long time.

Pokemon trading cards were an addendum to the video game put out by Nintendo, perhaps the company's most successful franchise after Mario Brothers. My son started collecting the cards, and they became an obsession. We went everywhere—Toys 'R' Us, KB Toys, specialty stores—to get those cards. Nintendo craftily made some of them very rare and hard to get, and there was fierce competition to get a complete set. I spent hours on eBay bidding for Pokemon cards, sometimes buying a set of twenty or more just to get one elusive card. One of my consulting clients had an equally obsessed son who was much further along in his collection, and she "persuaded" him to give up some of his rare duplicates. Simultaneously, a contact in Japan sent me Pokemon cards that hadn't even been released in the United States, and for a brief while, I was a hero. I basked in the glory, but it was short-lived.

The Cabbage Patch Kids are long gone; there may be Tamagotchis in the house, but I don't know where they are; and I bet my son doesn't know where his Pokemon cards are either. The emotional energy and real dollars lavished on them are gone—a distant, fading memory.

All of these once desperately wanted objects were within a certain time, and *nothing* within time will give you any enduring satisfaction or happiness. It all rusts or fades or corrodes and disappears sooner or later. And everything you're chasing now is within time.

The young man, Nachiketa, saw his father, a learned sage, give away cattle that were infirm and dry and chided him for giving such poor alms. "To whom will you give me away?" he mocked, and his father, in anger, snapped, "To Death do I give you."

So Nachiketa went to the abode of the king of death and waited outside for three days for him to arrive. Death was overjoyed to see such a fine specimen and promptly offered him three boons—one for each of the days he'd spent without receiving traditional hospitality.

For his first boon, Nachiketa asked that his father get over his anger and greet him with love. It was granted. For his second boon, he requested instruction about a ritual that enabled the performer to reach heaven, and that too was granted.

For his third boon, he asked about the secret of death and everlasting life. Death hesitated at that and made him a counteroffer—many counteroffers. Death offered him vast wealth, kingdoms with boundless land, thousands of cattle and horses and elephants, beauteous maidens to sing and dance and entertain him in all ways, children and grandchildren blessed with long life and high intelligence, and whatever else his heart could desire.

Each time Nachiketa asked, "Will this give me bliss that never ends?" and each time Death had to answer, "No, it lasts a long time, but one day, it will come to an end." The youth turned down all of the counteroffers and insisted on his boon being granted.

Death praised Nachiketa for his persistence and wisdom in rejecting transitory pleasures and instructed him on what brings lasting bliss and deep happiness that never ends.

What did Death reveal to our hero? I'll tell you shortly, but play along with me for a while first and do the following exercise.

□

it all passes by sooner or later

Look back over your life beginning with your earliest memories. What is the first thing you recall wanting desperately? Did you get it? And the next and the next? Pick at least three things you wanted that you actually obtained. Did you expect lasting pleasure, and did you get it? What are you striving for now—money, power, fame? See that this, even if you do get some or all of it, will also gradually fade away. Browse the twenty-year-old archives of any business magazine. Look at the cover photographs of the people profiled. They were once movers and shakers, household names. You may not even recognize some of their names today. They are yesterday's stories and fading fast.

Many have noted the transitory nature of earthly accomplishment. In Chapter 17, you read about Ozymandias and Julius Caesar, the mighty emperor turned to clay.

Now consider this verse by James Shirley, who expresses the same sentiment in different words:

The glories of our blood and state
Are shadows, not substantial things;
There is no armour against Fate;
Death lays his icy hand on kings:
Sceptre and Crown
Must tumble down,
And in the dust be equal made
With the poor crooked scythe and spade.

When you understand this very clearly and deeply, you will observe changes in your attitude and the things you strive for.

▣

So what was the secret of everlasting happiness that Death revealed to the bold youth? It is the knowledge you gained in

Chapter 20, that there is an underlying unity in all people and things. You may know this intellectually, but you don't really "grok" it. For those not familiar with Robert A. Heinlein's delightful work *Stranger in a Strange Land*, here is how one of the characters explains the term:

"Grok" means to understand so thoroughly that the observer becomes part of the observed—to merge, blend, intermarry, lose identity in group experience. . . . If I chopped you up and made a stew, you and the stew, whatever was in it, would grok—and when I ate you, we would grok together and nothing would be lost and it would not matter which one of us did the eating.

The concept itself is quite difficult to grok!

When you grok that unity, you find that you're at the place you were seeking and, indeed, were there all along.

24

It's your model—not reality!!

☐

A MENTAL MODEL IS a notion you have of how the world works. And you have many models—certainly dozens, probably hundreds. Do you, for example, believe that the way to get ahead is to work hard, come to the office early and stay late, take the initiative and do projects that aren't really part of your duties, try to be noticed favorably by your boss and her boss, and constantly study so that you're always abreast of your field and growing professionally?

Recognize that this is a model you hold. It's not "reality," although the odds are good that you think it is. It doesn't, for example, allow for the person who was hired at a very senior level of a major investment bank because he was a world-class bridge player.

You have a model for anything and everything—one for determining how to interact with your boss, another for how to treat your spouse, yet another for selecting which movie to see or which restaurant to eat at. Your model for picking a restaurant may call for asking close friends for a recommendation. Your spouse's model may be to browse the Web to check out the highest-rated establishment serving the type of cuisine you desire. These are two different models. They're not mutually exclusive, and you may well use both of them at some time or other.

The funny thing about mental models is that the more you invest in one, the more firmly you believe in whatever model you're using, the more "evidence" you get that the universe actually behaves in the way you think it does.

═══

The village chief rested for a couple of hours each afternoon, and it was his custom to receive visitors at this time. Any person who wished to settle in the village was required to meet with the chief. He did not have legal authority to prevent anyone from actually taking up residence in the community, but he did have great influence and wasn't hesitant about using it. The village was a peaceful, tolerant place where inhabitants went out of their way to help each other, and he wanted to keep it that way.

One day, he met with a burly individual who wanted to buy a farm and settle down. "Tell me, my son, why you wish to come here," he said.

"Well," said the man, "this seems like a prosperous village. The land is fertile, and the climate tolerable. The only thing I don't know is the nature of the people. What are they like?"

"That's a good question," said the chief. "Before I answer, tell me about the people in the village you left."

"Terrible," said the man without hesitation. "They were jealous of me because my crops were lush and took every opportunity to steal from me. I couldn't trust anyone. They would deceive me and rob me blind were it not for the care I took to be on my guard."

"My son," said the chief, shaking his head in sorrow, "this is not the right place for you to come after the hardship you have endured. The people here are exactly like that. They will take every advantage they can of you and leave you stranded. I hope you haven't committed to buying the farm you were looking at. If you have, I can use my influence to get your deposit back. You need a place more in tune with your nature."

The man thanked the chief, accepted his offer to help, and left the village the next day.

Shortly thereafter, the chief met an older and slightly more impoverished farmer who also was thinking of putting down roots in the village and posed him the same query.

"What can I say, good sir," exclaimed the man. "The village I left was like heaven. No one ever had friendlier neighbors. They outdid each other to be of help to anyone who suffered the slightest misfortune. I would trust them with anything, even my life."

"Why then did you leave?" queried the chief.

"Alas! My land was leased, and the landlord's son wished to return to the village, so he refused to extend my term," lamented the farmer. "I would have bought a smaller farm if I could have, but everyone wants to live there, and the price was more than I could afford."

"I have splendid news for you, my friend," beamed the chief. "The people in this village are exactly like that. You will find a wonderful home here. I have a good friend who will lease you several acres if I tell him to, and I will make sure that you can buy it on easy terms if you work diligently and prove yourself."

===

That's pretty much the way it works. The universe reflects back to you what you send out. You look at what comes your way, and this gives you confirmation that what you thought and sent out was the "truth."

Don't make the mistake of trying to establish whether your mental models are "true" or "false." At some level, they are all true, and on another level, they are all false. Depending on the predilection with which you start, you'll find plenty of corroboration for each.

It is much better for you to look at whether or not your mental model is working for you. Do you feel stuck in any part of your life? If it seems as if you are swimming through molasses and nothing seems to be going right, then assuredly one or more of your mental models are not serving you well.

In an exercise I conduct in my programs, I take participants through a process where they actually identify the mental model they are using and then evaluate how well this model is serving them. One attractive woman—whom many felt had a shell around her—finally buttoned down the model she was using to interact with people:

- Always keep your guard up. People are not to be trusted, and almost everyone you run into (especially of the male persuasion) wants something from you and is devious.

- The best way to prevent people from taking whatever it is they want to take from you is by backhanded meanness.

Don't openly avoid people or let them believe that you're unkind. Simply pretend, in the shallowest way, to be nice and hope they realize that you don't like talking to them by your lack of eye contact and unwillingness to laugh at their jokes.

◨ Avoid people you don't like at all costs. Don't say "hi" to them, and don't stay in touch with them.

◨ Never truly let people know how much you don't trust them. Pretend to trust them, but *keep your guard up*!

◨ Everyone is selfish, devious, and unkind by nature.

She had good reason to believe that her model was accurate. At least, she thought she had good reason. She was passing through a particularly troubled phase in her personal life, and male colleagues—some of whom barely knew her—constantly hit on her and made insensitive comments. There was tension in group situations she was a part of, a sort of underground hostility, and despite her physical loveliness, she was often left completely alone.

As she went through my program, she decided to consciously adopt another model, one that she thought she would merely "test" for a while so she could prove to herself that it was "wrong." Here is the one she came up with:

◨ Be kind to everyone. You never know what lies beneath the surface, and most flaws you notice in others are simply further manifestations of your own flaws, so don't be critical.

◨ Everyone has beauty within; you just have to look for it.

▣ The best way to find that beauty is through sincere concern and thought. Let your own guard down, and people will let you in. Be sincere, and true friendships will arise.

▣ No one is out to get you! Trust everyone.

▣ Everyone really only lives within himself or herself, so you don't have a responsibility to create your friends' worlds. Just support them.

▣ Love is all around, just look and you'll find it. Everyone is kind and gentle by nature.

To her surprise, she found mountains of "evidence" to show that this was the way things "really" were! Her experience of life was so much better with the second model that she simply adopted it permanently. Suddenly when teams were being formed at work, groups got into tugs-of-war to obtain her.

▣

how to change your mental model

Consciously changing your mental model is a powerful technique, but it may take some trial and error before you arrive at a model that truly works for you and transforms your life. You'll find it much easier and faster if you bear the lessons of Chapters 20 through 22 in mind.

Pick any area of your life—say relationships. Select a person with whom you have troubled interactions. Clearly recollect the last few dealings you had with this person. Now consciously acknowledge that she has the same desire you do. That she too wants to avoid suffering and be happy. Possibly, in her world, you are the cause of much sorrow. See that she, like you, is acting out a role and identifying with it. By doing this, you are taking the first step toward acknowledging that you're the actor, not the character. Next recognize that you are both human beings stuck in your respective predicaments and see what you can do to be of service to her.

Record how you feel as you do this and afterward.

▣

25

Quiet the tumultuous horde!

□

BLAISE PASCAL, THE French scientist and philosopher, reportedly observed that we bring all of our miseries on ourselves by our simple inability to sit quietly in a room by ourselves. Peter Drucker was well known as a management theorist, but he also had a keen understanding of the human predicament. The following observation is uncannily accurate:

In a few hundred years, when the history of our time will be written from a long-term perspective, it is likely that the most important event historians will see is not technology, not the Internet, not e-commerce. It is an unprecedented change in the human condition. For the first time—literally—substantial and rapidly growing numbers of people have choices. For the first time, they will have to manage themselves. And society is totally unprepared for it.

Chapter 6 touched on our inability to manage ourselves, to sit quietly by ourselves. That incapacity leads to frenetic action, to the cultivation of all kinds of ever-more-complex wants and heroic undertakings to satisfy them.

——

Larry achieved the very pinnacle of success, or he thought he had, when he became CEO of a large conglomerate. But the happiness he thought would come never did. Yes, there was an initial thrill of gratification, but that was extremely short-lived as workers in six countries went on a coordinated wildcat strike.

When he dug the company out of that one, he had to deal with multiple suicide bomb attacks on trains that transported his goods in Southeast Asia. Then there was the breakdown of key machinery that halted production on two continents.

And then there were the people. Everyone wanted to talk to Larry personally. He had known that, as the leader of a well-known company, he would have social obligations, but he was unprepared for the sheer volume of those who wanted face time with him or the persistence with which they went about trying to get it. Employees, shareholders, analysts, journalists, politicians, fund-raisers for various causes, customers, social activists, and community organizers—the list was endless.

He became more "efficient" and divided his time into smaller slices. He scheduled appointments for five minutes each and even planned thirty-second bathroom breaks. He got used to functioning at this pace, then he retired and his world came apart.

Larry tried golf but it didn't hold his attention. What had been a wonderful, relaxing activity when he was a CEO on the links with important clients became dry and distasteful when he was part of a club foursome. His wife threw him out of the house because she didn't like him puttering around during the day and messing up the kitchen.

In despair, he sought a meeting with a sage. At the appointed hour, he knocked on the door and was asked to enter. He did.

"Out," said the sage wrathfully. "There is no room here for such a crowd."

"What crowd?" Larry questioned, puzzled.

"I gave you permission to meet me," said the sage, still nettled. "I did not ask you to bring your wife, your board members, your children, your unemployed nephew, your deadbeat brother, and the rest of the horde. Go away and come back when you are alone."

Larry was nothing if not persistent; he promptly saw this as a new challenge and rose to meet it. He came again the next day and the next and the next and the next. He came every day for a month, and each time, the holy man refused him entrance.

One day, he became annoyed himself. "There is no one with me today," he exclaimed.

"True," said the wise man, instantly understanding what he meant. "But you are bringing things with you. And my hut is too small for all that you are trying to drag in. It's all part of the crowd."

Larry knew that the sage was right; he still had his crowd with him, and it showed no sign of thinning. "How can I get rid of this throng?" he finally pleaded.

The sage taught him what to do, and he went home and practiced it diligently. It took him many months, but one day he knocked again on the sage's door. He was told to enter, and the sage did not send him away but instead asked him to take a seat.

What was true of that hapless executive is true of you. Become conscious of the army you are lugging around with you each day. See how each person or thing clamors for attention and fights with other people and things to get it. Want more proof? Have you ever been introduced to someone and ten seconds later can't remember her name? Have you ever started listening to a favorite song and suddenly realized that it had ended while your thoughts were elsewhere? Have you ever been driving and overshot your exit because you were preoccupied? Have you ever forgotten to mail a letter or buy an item your spouse requested or run an important errand?

If any of these is true of you, you're carrying a burden. Possibly (probably), you've been carrying it around so long that you no longer even know you're doing so. You're weighted down with your memories, your desires and hopes, your fears and aversions. You lack the ability to live in the present as you flit between the near and distant pasts and your visions of tomorrow and the day after.

No wonder you're so tired. If you were to approach the sage, he would turn you away as well. So what did he tell the executive, and can you avail of this advice as well?

Sure, you can. Practice the following exercise diligently.

▣

eschew multitasking; try mindfulness instead

Recognize that information overload and attention deficit have become the norm today. One way people try to cope with this situation is by multitasking. You probably do it too, and you may even consider it a strength. Many job postings list "ability to multitask" as a requirement, and some employers consider it admirable.

Disabuse yourself of this idea. Multitasking simply means that you do many things badly and take much more time at it. You'll discover this for yourself.

Begin by doing this exercise in twenty-minute intervals; you will gradually increase to two-hour spans. Pick any task that you have to get accomplished and gather everything you need to work on it. Turn off your e-mail. Shut down your Web browser unless it is necessary for the task at hand. If it is, keep only those windows that are relevant open. Don't have the radio or television on. Turn off the phone if you can.

Visualize what you have to do and slow down your breathing. Get down to ten breaths a minute or even fewer—deep abdominal breaths, not shallow chest breathing.

Note the time and commence your task with complete attention. Don't allow any distraction to take away your focus. Remember that "hurry" is in your mind. Work unhurriedly, but as fast as you are able. Imagine yourself as a container of golden energy and pour yourself into the task. Thoughts— many of them—will come into your head unbidden. Some of them will seem urgent, and the demands will be incessant. Observe all of them calmly and let them go. Don't get carried away by any of them. If a particularly useful idea strikes you, note it down on a pad so you don't forget it, then let it go.

Do this for twenty minutes and give yourself a five-minute break. Then repeat.

When you actually try it, you'll discover that this seemingly simple exercise is a lot tougher than it appears. There will be many occasions when you "fail," when you discover that you've drifted off in a hazy cloud and the minutes have ticked by unnoticed. Simply note this as an indication of how far you have to go and get down to it again. Do not—I repeat *not*—beat yourself up. That is simply more drama you create, and it distracts you from the task at hand.

You'll discover that, as you practice, you accomplish a great deal more than you normally do and with less effort. Celebrate this discovery. This relaxed focus is "mindfulness." Cultivate it but don't try to be mindful all the time. You will not succeed, and your perceived failure could actually take you on a downward spiral.

You want to get to the stage where you can, at will, become mindful for a twenty-minute span. Once you get there, increase it to thirty minutes. Go up in increments of ten minutes until you can be continuously mindful for two hours. Stop.

As you do this exercise, you'll notice that the crowd you're carrying around thins. Celebrate this. They all come back later, but you now know you can banish them, and this knowledge will give you many future victories.

Extend this practice deliberately to all areas of your life. Notice how superficial many interactions are. Have you ever had a colleague wish you "good morning" and be halfway down the hall before you could reply? Do you do this yourself?

When you say, "Good morning," really mean it. Establish eye contact, and say it with energy and from your heart. Wish the person every good fortune and blessing. Do it silently and sincerely. Do it to people with whom you have casual interactions, such as the cashier at the cafeteria or your cab driver, and do it to people who are important in your life, such as your spouse or boss.

Again, do this many times consciously, but don't expect to be able to do it all the time. You'll notice that the nature of your interactions with others changes. Relationships become deeper. Conversations happen that didn't before. Celebrate this as well.

If you're diligent in your practice, and as you become more proficient, you'll observe that many members of your gaggle have left for good. Exercises in later chapters will drive even more away.

回

26

The question itself
is irrelevant!

◨

ROM TIME TO time, you ask yourself questions and receive no answers. Some of them are heartfelt questions, and they arise from deep anguish and empathy for others: *Why is there so much suffering in the world? Why do people butcher each other with such barbarity? Why are the affluent so indifferent to the plight of so many people who live in abject misery?* At other times, the questions are more personal but no less fervent: *Why, oh why, do such things constantly happen to me?*

These questions come from the very depth of your being. Sometimes it feels as if you're being split in two and they are emerging from the fissure, born from pain—an ache that's everywhere and won't go away. These are insistent questions, and you seek hard for explanations but don't find any. So you go back to your life dissatisfied and bury your unease in frantic activity.

You'll never find the answers to such insistent questions. In fact, there are no answers. You're looking for solutions in the plane of logic and cause and effect, and there is no panacea in this realm. Einstein moved from three-dimensional space to four-dimensional space-time in his general theory of relativity to explain phenomena that had been observed but not understood. String theorists now postulate even more dimensions in their quest for a theory that unifies all known forces of nature.

In similar fashion, you have to move to a higher state of consciousness if you really want to ease your pain permanently instead of papering over it with insistent action. In this higher state, you won't find the answers you're seeking; the questions themselves will drop away and become irrelevant.

Puzzled? Perhaps a story is in order.

═══

You have an extraordinarily vivid dream, a nightmare so dramatic that you still recall every detail. You and your wife are on a luxury cruise when pirates capture your ship. All the people in penthouse suites are swiftly transferred to fast motorboats and ferried away. You and your wife are among them.

The days that follow are agonizing, filled with torment. You're beaten and kicked and slammed against the wall. You're injected with heroin as the kidnappers try to get you addicted. You know you have at least two broken ribs, because they scrape against each other and the pain is excruciating. You learn to walk stiff legged, with your back in a specific position to avoid disturbing the bones.

The pirates quickly discover that you love your wife dearly and use that to manipulate you. They break her finger to get you to reveal the password on your ATM card. You would have given it to them freely, but they injured her anyway and did it with sadistic pleasure. It's a desperate situation.

All prisoners are held separately in makeshift cells, but it is an improvised arrangement, not a real prison, and there are plenty of opportunities for you to talk with each other. The pirates try to prevent this by the threat of severe beatings if you are discovered, and they deliver on this often enough that all of you spend most of your time in sullen silence. One day, one of your shipboard friends sidles up to you. One of the pirates has been bribed and will let all of you go—he needs a million dollars up front as earnest money and an equal amount later when you're out of the prison and close to the boat that he has arranged to take you to safety. He'll also accompany you, because his life will be forfeit if he remains. Can you arrange for a million dollars to reach him today?

It so happens that you can. You do business in many countries and sometimes grease the skids by buying off influential politicians. So you have developed a method of arranging cash transfers that don't leave an accounting trail and depend on code words that have specific meaning. You reveal what your shipmate needs to know to get your office manager to release the money to the pirate, who has a numbered account in a Swiss bank. These are sophisticated pirates, and you marvel at how the world has changed.

Events move fast. Hours before you are to make your escape, one of the pirates kicks you viciously in the knee. You can no longer walk, but you urge the others to leave anyway and take good care of your wife. You so want her to escape from this hell. You watch anxiously as the others leave with their clearly frightened pirate turncoat.

Minutes later, you hear gunfire, machine gun bursts and explosions that may be grenades. You see men in military uniforms running toward your cage and taking cover. There is fire somewhere—you can see columns of smoke rising to the sky from a building just outside your line of sight.

You are beside yourself with worry. Did they make it? Is your wife safe? You heard a woman screaming desperately—was that your wife? For Pete's sake, what's happening out there? You can't imagine life without her.

The door to your cell is kicked open, and two men rush in. Both are carrying guns—pistols in belt holsters and AK-47s in their hands. One of them is the pirate captain.

"*You!*" he screams, looking at you with bloodshot eyes. "You brought them here." He grabs you by the collar and throws you on the floor. You shout as your different injuries hurt simultaneously. Seeing your awkward knee, he smiles maliciously and lifts his foot. He is wearing army boots, and he brings one down on your injured knee with all his weight.

You scream. The pain is so intense that . . . you wake up!

═══

Once you're awake, do you try to go back and see if your wife made it out safely? What happened to that question, the question you were so desperate to know the answer to?

▣

be the actor, not the character

Go back and read Chapter 17 again. You're the actor, not the character. The role you're playing, the difficulties you're experiencing—these belong to the character, not the actor. See yourself relishing the role and playing it with gusto. Is the character being hit with unusual buffets? Wonderful! It's a complicated and nuanced role that will allow you, the actor, to demonstrate your exceptional talent. You gird your loins and prepare to give the very best performance of which you're capable.

Can you adopt this model? It will stand you in exceptionally good stead if you can.

▣

27

It's not fair!

□

WHEN YOU WAKE up from your nightmare experience, you find that the world is a wonderful place. It always has been; it always will be. When you wake up, you're anchored in the unity proclaimed by so many mystics in different traditions. The underlying oneness of everything is no longer an intellectually satisfying model but an integral part of who you are—it has been baked into you. The concepts from Chapter 20 are not strange and far out; they're your commonplace experience.

The bad news is that waking up is both incredibly simple and unbelievably difficult. The cerebral understanding is easy, but to be steeped in it involves the extinction of the ego, which is not something that's likely to happen tomorrow.

The good news is that even a rudimentary sense that this is actually the way things are and a determination, however imperfect, to traverse that route will completely turn your life around and propel you into an infinitely more pleasant realm. Sometimes, as in the following story, the seeming injustice of the world is the spur that leads to awakening.

===

The Golden Squirrel was hurrying along the forest path when she came across a brigand. The police who had apprehended him had left him there while they went to the nearby river to rest and eat. They weren't about to share their meager supply of food with him. He was trussed up and not going to go anywhere.

"Save me," the brigand begged the Golden Squirrel. "These are renegade police officers, and my life is forfeit if they get me to their station."

"What have you done that they have arrested you?" inquired the Golden Squirrel.

"I have done nothing evil," answered the brigand. "I was a bonded laborer. My master was unjust and used to beat me, so one day I broke loose from my chains and thrashed him before running away. For this, I was branded an outlaw. I've been in the deepest forest ever since and am the leader of a group of people who've been similarly mistreated. We were safe until these rogues in uniform, who are really bounty hunters, came to know our whereabouts. Please free me, and I will look after you forever."

So piteously did he recount his tale that the Golden Squirrel was moved, and she gnawed through the ropes that bound him. Quickly, he scooped her up and vanished into the jungle, back to his house.

The brigand was true to his word and looked after the squirrel well. Freed of the necessity to forage, she became fat and slow. One day, the brigand's wife grabbed her and put her in a cage. The brigand remonstrated with his wife, but she shut him up brusquely. "The flesh of the Golden Squirrel is tasty beyond belief, and she will be my lunch tomorrow," declared the wife. "You can have some too, but don't you dare interfere." So to keep the peace, the brigand acquiesced.

"I saved your life," the Golden Squirrel reminded him. "How can you do this to me? It's not fair."

"That's true," agreed the brigand. "But there is no justice in the world. That's the way life is. Ask anyone if you don't believe me."

The Golden Squirrel looked at the goat grazing nearby, and it nodded its head sadly. "I give them milk, yet they beat me. When I run dry, they will cut my throat and eat me. It's true that there is no justice in the world."

The squirrel looked at the serving maid, and she also shook her head. "I had a family and a house once," she said, "but the brigand killed my husband and stole my child. Now I'm a servant. I dare not run away because I don't know where my child is, and the brigand will kill him if I leave. There is definitely no justice in the world."

The Golden Squirrel's heart sank as she realized the perfidy of the man she had saved. "See?" said the thief as he hung up the cage. "That's the way life is. I would have kept you well, but since you're going to die anyway, I might as well grab a morsel of you for myself. I too have heard that your flesh is tasty, and there is more of it now than when you came." And he laughed shamelessly.

That night, the servant came silently to the cage and opened the door. She picked up the Golden Squirrel and placed her gently on the ground. "Run away, little one," she said. "There is no justice in the world, but sometimes there is a little balance."

"Come with me," entreated the little creature. "They'll know you did this and will kill you."

"No, little one," replied the maid. "I can't flee for fear of what will befall my son. They'll beat me, but they won't kill me because I'm useful to them. This is my fate, and I will suffer it. Run away now."

Some months later, the Golden Squirrel chanced on a party of policemen. From their conversation, she divined that they were the ones who had captured the brigand and were still looking for him.

"Would you like me to lead you to him?" she volunteered. "I can take you by a back path that no one knows about, and it is unguarded."

So the policemen followed the squirrel and burst in on the unsuspecting gang. There was a brief but fierce fight, and all the brigands were captured. During the melee, one of the policemen emerged from a hut with an infant, and the serving woman recognized her son. She rushed toward him, and the policeman, mistaking her intent, swung his stave and broke her neck. She died without holding her son, who became an orphan.

"It's so unfair," muttered the Golden Squirrel as she left the scene. "There really is no justice in this world."

===

In the words of Anthony DeMello, Jesuit priest and enlightened seer, "There is no explanation you can give that would explain away all the sufferings and evil and torture and destruction and hunger in the world! You'll never explain it. You can try gamely with your formulas, religious and otherwise, but you'll never explain it. Because life is a mystery, which means your thinking mind cannot make sense of it. For that you've got to wake up and then you'll suddenly realize that reality is not the problem, you are the problem."

For some of you, this will make immediate and profound sense. If so, let it sink in. Meditate on it.

For others, this will appear stupid and may even arouse anger and hostility. If this happens, move on to the next chapter. Don't give vent to your ill feeling. Be open to the possibility that, sometime in the future, it will become clearer.

▣

the journey is all there is

Albert Einstein famously said that the significant problems in the world can't be solved at the same level of consciousness in which we created them. All of life is a journey to reach a higher level of consciousness. Think about where you are on the continuum of consciousness. Plot what you'll do to make progress, but recognize even as you plan that none of it is within your control. Remember, you need to invest in the process, not the outcome.

▣

28

The root of all your problems

□

READY TO MOVE on? OK, here's a statement that may startle you. There is one characteristic you have, a single trait, that causes the vast majority of all the problems you face. More precisely, all the problems you think you face. I said *trait*, but if you want to think of it as a defect, go right ahead. It's really pernicious.

I've already talked about this, but let's examine it in more detail now. This disastrous habit is your tendency to be "me-centered." You interpret all events, near and far, in terms of their impact on "me." You live in a world where you are the center of the universe, and the planets, sun, other stars, and galaxies all rotate around you.

Think about how every action you take, every thought you indulge, even your instinctive reactions to all events are soaked through and dripping with self-interest. There's nothing you do that doesn't reek of your desire to rearrange the world to suit your convenience.

I have deliberately used strong and provocative language. Do you find yourself seething with anger and bristling with hostility? Hold on for just a moment and consider the following:

- ☐ Do you quickly, almost instantaneously, evaluate each person you meet and then behave in a fashion that reflects your likes and dislikes? Do you laugh louder at the jokes of a millionaire and forgive his social gaffes? No, no, you don't expect anything from him. It's not as blatant as that. It's simply a subtle way of communicating that you're open to further discourse. You're also more attentive to those you find sexually attractive and people who are famous.

- ☐ Do you seek out the company of people who delight you? Who tell you how good you are and stroke that fragile ego of yours? Do you avoid people who grate on you? Who are ill-mannered and tell you you're not as wonderful as you think you are?

- ☐ Do you get irritated at the boor who talks too loudly on his cell phone during your commute, or the rude lout who rests his shoe on the seat next to you?

- ☐ If your spouse gets a great job offer, your best friend wins the $10 million lottery, your father-in-law is transferred to another country, or a hundred similar events, do you instinctively and instantly think of how it will affect you?

These are just a few of the ways in which you're trying to engineer the world into what you would like it to be. Please understand, there's *nothing* wrong with trying to do that. As long as you occupy your human body, you have to do something to fill your time. You have a mind, it has preferences, so you might as well try to humor your druthers. There's no problem here. The problem lies in your attaching your well-being to your success in these efforts.

Go back once again, this time to Chapters 13 and 14. You are back in the thrall of the if-then model. As I showed there, the model itself is fallacious. It's not what you try for that's "wrong." Nothing that you try for is wrong in that sense, although you obviously want to think seriously about anything that is illegal, immoral, or unethical. What *is* wrong is the notion that if you succeed in your particular rearrangement, you will be happier. Success may well bring you a temporary thrill that you mistake for more "happiness," but the feeling soon passes, and you begin the weary quest all over again.

Here is an instructive tale that appears in some form or other in many traditions:

===

He was a mighty emperor who could have whatever he wanted. Astute generals and mighty armies were his to command. Squads of servitors were ready to jump to his wishes. Courtesans and jesters waited to amuse him if summoned. But still he was unsettled. He was subject to mood swings, and the range of these was epic.

One of his generals won a mighty victory over a longtime enemy, and the emperor was thrilled beyond measure. Two days later, his favorite queen was stricken with a dreadful, possibly terminal disease, and he was plunged into despair. His wife recovered; the defeated king knelt before him, paid tribute, and swore loyalty; and the emperor beamed. He learned that his recovered queen was now barren and his successor would have to be the son of his second queen, whom he despised, and the world weighed heavy on him again.

And so it went on, day after day, year after year. He would be up, and he would be down. It seemed that, despite his power and wealth, he was down more often and with greater intensity. Somehow he knew this was wrong. Life was not meant to be like this. So he sent for the head priest of the temple, a man of great wisdom and spiritual accomplishment. His father had never made any important decision without soliciting the views of the priest, but the present emperor had departed from this practice.

"Tell me," beseeched the monarch. "Tell me what I must do so I am not chained to this vale of sorrow, fluctuating between exhilaration and depression like a ball tossed to and fro between small children at play."

The old man looked at the troubled emperor with compassion. "Your Majesty, you have fallen far from the understanding you had when you came to me for lessons in your younger days," he said sorrowfully. "You have traveled so long and hard on the path of darkness and unbridled sensual enjoyment that it will be eons before you can regain the distance you have lost and again reach your lost position on the path of light. However, this particular problem has an easy solution."

"Tell me," said the emperor eagerly. "Instruct me so that I may be at ease."

"Come to me at the temple tomorrow," said the holy man. "I will give you a scroll. Anytime you are confronted with a problem, anytime you are feted and praised, read this scroll and ponder its message. Do not do this casually, but think deeply about it. If you do, it will reveal its secret to you." He turned and strode out.

So the ruler went to the temple, obtained the scroll, and did as he was bidden. A great change came over him. It began slowly, but then it gathered momentum, and his subjects were amazed at the transformation in him. No longer was he subject to tantrums and arbitrary dispensations of punishments and favors. His temperament was equable and his judgment reasoned. So great a monarch did he become that there was universal bemoaning when he left this world.

After a brief period of mourning, his son took the throne and, with great curiosity, unfurled the scroll. "Truly there is great wisdom here," he reflected, as he contemplated the four words that were written there.

They said, "This, too, shall pass."

=

Some people are blatantly, ruthlessly, unsparingly me-centered. They are hypercompetitive, driven individuals who have to win every hand and never leave any money on the table. They drive others hard and themselves even harder as they strive to remake their neck of the woods in a manner to their liking, and their egos are huge. They frequently reach positions of power and influence and bask in the adulation of a society in which material success is envied. They glory in this and try to get more, going faster and even faster on the treadmill. Perhaps they, like the young man in Chapter 23, should ask themselves if this—whatever the "this" is—will give lasting happiness.

Odds are good that you're not like that. You recognize that you're me-centered much of the time but probably take pride in your altruistic inclinations as well. You do things for other people. You contribute to charities. If there's a disaster in some part of the world, you call the help line and give something. You may even volunteer for some worthy cause on a regular basis. You're a decent citizen working to do your bit to make the world a better place.

But even with all this, the me-centered streak is alive and well, just in a different form. You seek approbation. You want people to think well of you and pat you on the back. You want to be recognized as a caring individual. You have an image of what a responsible person is like, and you strive to make your actions fit this mold. It's important for your self-image.

What's wrong with living in a me-centered world? Nothing, nothing at all. But if you spend the vast majority of your time living in a me-centered universe, you'll be depressed, dejected, anguished, disconsolate, and downhearted much of the time. That's just the way it is. You try to achieve happiness by overtly grabbing stuff for yourself in a ruthlessly competitive manner, and whether you succeed or not, you'll get knocked on the head. You do the same thing in a subtler fashion by being less obvious and more charitable; you'll still get knocked on the head, but perhaps less severely.

In my programs, women of Asian origin who vehemently disagree with the preceding statement sometimes accost me. Many come from cultures where they are the caregivers for the generations before and after them, and they feel emotionally burnt out. This is especially true of those who are also highly educated and professionally qualified. In their view, the problem in their life is that they haven't been taking sufficient care of themselves and actually need to become more me-centered. This is also the beef of some parents who feel worn out after years of caring "for" their children. They feel they've been far too "other-centered" and need to be more me-centered and look after themselves.

Actually, all of these people are living squarely in a me-centered world and need to step out of it! They don't recognize that they're me-centered, but that is exactly what they are. Let me explain. The women come from a milieu where there are cultural expectations, and they are well regarded if they conform to those expectations. So they try to fit in by overtly putting the welfare of others ahead of their own, even while resenting this inwardly. Over time, this divergence between feeling and action becomes a mass of seething resentment that eventually boils over. Similarly, the parents have fixed notions of how their children should behave for "their own good" and try to force them into this model. They expect the universe to conform to their views and suffer if it doesn't. They never recognize that they cause their own suffering.

When you try to gain acceptance and admiration by behaving in a manner expected by others, when you try to mold the behavior of others in accordance with your notion of what's right, you're being me-centered. And sooner or later, this leads to pain.

There is a balance here, and that's what you frequently don't recognize. Yes, you do need to fit into your social framework. Yes, as a parent, you do have a duty to teach your child and educate her according to your best understanding. But when what you do is a burden that weighs you down rather than a labor of love, and you carry on because of your desire for acceptance and approbation, that is merely a different form of me-centered behavior! And it will inevitably lead to a feeling of ennui and emptiness. That's simply the way it is.

The way out is to practice living in an other-centered universe.

◫

step into an other-centered universe

Carefully and keenly observe how much of your time you spend in a me-centered universe. Notice the spurt of irritation when you're hurrying along and find your way blocked by a big, slow-moving individual. The annoyance when an elderly, befuddled lady takes forever to pay the cashier and painstakingly puts the change back in her wallet. And the way you stew when your pompous colleague drones on and on in an office meeting.

See how many of your interactions are superficial. Do you say, "Good morning" as a cursory greeting and walk on before the other person even has a chance to reply?

Slow down. When you say, "Good morning," sincerely wish the person every blessing. Do this silently as you make eye contact and hold it. Imagine you're a searchlight capable of beaming out goodwill and benisons. Direct this powerful light at people with whom you interact.

Experiment with this mental model: "It is my duty and privilege to be of service. I will do whatever I can to make life easier for all people who cross my path—boss, colleagues, family members, friends, and random people like the one who stops me on the street to ask for directions."

Don't expect anything in return, not even a thank-you. The slightest hint of expectation destroys much of the power of this exercise. Rather than expecting thanks, be thankful that you've been given an opportunity to be of service.

See how, as you really get into the spirit of the exercise, good feelings arise in you in great gushes. It may take some time, but they will come.

Also, be warned that's extremely difficult to hold on to this model all the time and with everyone. Don't even try. Do dedicate several intervals each day to being other-centered. Do pick specific people to whom you can be of service with no thought of self. Do a little bit more each week, and don't beat up on yourself for not being more successful in this task.

◘

Some very bright people have taken my programs and have gleefully pointed out the flaw in the exercise. Their argument runs like this: "If I'm being other-centered so I can stop feeling lousy about myself and start moving toward the vision you laid out, aren't I really being me-centered all the time?"

These are perceptive individuals, and they're absolutely correct. Yes, you are indeed being me-centered when you start doing this exercise in order to feel better. But this is merely a starting phase. When you've done it long enough, it becomes a part of you. Then you're no longer trying to be other-centered to achieve anything but because you've become a person who behaves this way naturally.

That's when you'll receive the greatest benefits from the exercise.

29

Is anything for real?

◎

A man will find that as he alters his thoughts towards things and other people, things and other people will alter towards him.

—JAMES ALLEN

AMERICAN BUDDHIST TEACHER Jack Kornfield relates a funny incident in his book *A Path with Heart*. He had just returned to the United States after many years of study in Buddhist monasteries in Thailand and Burma (now Myanmar). His head was shaved, and he was dressed in the loose, flowing robes of a Buddhist monk. Fresh from a life of many hours of daily meditation, he let the frenetic energy of New York City pass him by.

He was to meet his sister-in-law in midtown Manhattan in front of Elizabeth Arden's; she'd been given a gift certificate for a full day of pampering, including facial, haircut, manicure, and more. Since she wasn't there, he entered the establishment and was directed to a waiting room inside. He sat on a comfortable couch for a few minutes, and then his training and instincts took over. He crossed his legs, closed his eyes, and started to meditate.

Dimly he became aware of a disturbance, voices, and laughter. A loud exclamation of "Is he for real?" brought him back to the world, and he opened his eyes. He was surrounded by a gaggle of women dressed in white gowns with green paste smeared thickly on their faces and their hair in curlers. He looked at them astonished, and the question that popped into his head was "Are they for real?"

When I read that story, I was reminded of something else. Back when I was going to college in India in the late sixties, virtually everyone was leftist. Capitalism was a dirty word and a misbegotten ideology, and if you really disliked someone and wanted to insult him, you called him a capitalist. I was nonpolitical but had loads of friends who were vehemently anticapitalist.

A few years later, in the United States, I was asked various times by different officials if I was—or ever had been—a communist. Communism was the unspeakable profanity and foul invective to be used against someone you loathed. I laughed and am still laughing.

Such things only happen when we live in a me-centered world. We're so sure that the way in which we view the world is the only right and proper one that we see those who deviate from it as misguided and those who completely diverge from it as aliens from Mars. Such thinking inevitably leads to the sharp polarization that occurs in many facets of life today, especially in politics and religion.

Kornfield, because of his training and intellect, recognized what was happening, and this incident played a role in launching him on his path of explaining Buddhism to a Western lay audience. We don't know what changes, if any, happened to the women in the salon.

The fundamental problem with living in a me-centered world is that it implacably prevents you from understanding the essential similarities between all people, as described in Chapters 20 and 21. So others either become mechanisms by which you can achieve your ends and reinforce your worldview or are obstacles to be circumvented or crushed. You forget that everyone you meet, everyone in the world, is a human being stuck in the same predicament, trying with their imperfect intellect to make sense of this immensely complicated firmament. Each person is thinking, "May I be happy. May I be free from sorrow now and evermore." The only difference between individuals is the way in which they believe they can achieve their personal quest for happiness. Some actively wish ill for others as part of this search.

So where does that leave you? If all worldviews are just models, should you consider them all equally valid? Won't this lead to moral relativism where any act can be justified by some stretch of imagination? Can (should) you have compassion for someone who's your enemy and actively tries to destroy you?

The right answer is that there is no right answer. What you do as an individual is a reflection of your state of consciousness. There's a story of a man, who, disgusted with the seditious views the Buddha was spreading, gave the Enlightened One a drink laced with poison. The Buddha drank it, knowing full well what it was, and blessed the man. The poison had no effect on him, and the man was launched on his own journey of awakening. But that tale is apocryphal, and the person was the Buddha. What is its relevance for you and me?

Much more important than what you do is who you are being as you do it. Let me repeat that. *Whatever action you take, be consciously aware of who you are as you take it.* Pay particular attention to the many ways in which self-interest creeps into your thinking. For example, you come home tired from work, and your five-year-old daughter complains to you about how your four-year-old son has spilled ketchup on her favorite doll. Your son, in turn, is mad that his sister won't let him play with her toy furniture set. You explode angrily at this mutual sniping. You are a frustrated parent. You're also a bad example.

Howard was a senior executive and absolutely hated delivering the results of 360-degree evaluations—where colleagues, bosses, subordinates, and others anonymously give their opinions about an individual—to his subordinates. This was especially true when the comments were negative, which meant there was a good chance the person would be let go. He realized that his thinking was entirely me-centered: *I hate doing this. Why do I have to do this? I would rather be working on increasing sales in my region.*

Howard decided to come to terms with it. He had responsibilities and was well compensated for them; this was just something that came with his position. He elected to focus entirely on the person with whom he was dealing and the impact it would have on her. Soon after, he had to speak to a young manager who had received terrible evaluations up and down the line. He meditated for a few minutes before the meeting and consciously let go of his own feelings of dislike for the task ahead. He thought with compassion of the possible effect the talk would have on the young woman and what he could do to soften the blow.

"I was honest with her," Howard said later. "I told her what the report said, what was good and what wasn't. I told her what I agreed with and what I didn't and what the implications were. I was candid that, unless there was dramatic improvement in three months, she would probably be asked to leave. I then asked her how this affected her and her family and what I could do to help."

The result surprised him. The subordinate burst into tears and said that no one had ever offered her such constructive advice. She asked if she could meet with him every two weeks to chart progress, and the executive agreed. Four years later, Howard had left the firm, but the subordinate was still there and doing well.

"Little that I said was different from previous similar meetings," he reflected. "But the emotional space from which I spoke was vastly different. I wasn't thinking of finishing off a distasteful task. I was concerned about how I could help a young person in trouble survive in a difficult environment. I didn't realize what an enormous difference this would make. It was a huge lesson for me and part of my own growth as a manager."

When you honestly, sincerely, completely, and mindfully have the intention of being of service to your fellow human beings, something magical happens in the way you experience the world. There's really no way to describe this—you just have to discover it for yourself.

Deep down, in some way, we all know this. All we need to do is remember it. I know this because of the way participants in my program react to Nipun Mehta.

Nipun Mehta is an unusual character—a *very* unusual character. A Berkeley engineer, he was on the tennis team and good enough that he took a year off to explore the possibility of turning professional. When he graduated, there were many avenues open to him for traditional success, including high-powered careers in consulting and investment banking. He turned them down because he was already marching to a different drummer.

Nipun's observation was that far too many of our interactions are transactions—money for products or services. Even when mutually beneficial and entered into freely, transactions impoverish the spirit. There is an indescribable joy in giving for the sake of giving, for doing something good for someone else with no hope or expectation of any kind of reward, not even a thank-you. He knew that was true, and he came up with a wonderful way to let others discover it for themselves.

With a small group of like-minded friends, he created CharityFocus (charityfocus.org), a nonprofit organization that provides an outlet for volunteers to help many different charitable entities by using technology effectively to coordinate their efforts.

Karma Kitchen is a splendid example of the many "gift economy" initiatives sparked by CharityFocus. You can enter

Karma Kitchen, open every Sunday in a restaurant close to the University of California at Berkeley campus, and be served a scrumptious three-course meal. The entire meal is a gift. Contributions from someone who has eaten there previously have already paid for your meal, and at the end of the meal, you're given an envelope to make a contribution for people who come after you. No one keeps tabs. Part of the attraction is that everyone who eats there is served unconditionally and with warmth, as if they are guests in a home. Second and third helpings are part of the fare, and, other than the chefs, everyone—kitchen staff, waiters, busboys, and dishwashers—is a volunteer. Karma Kitchen has covered its costs and then some from its first day, and several members of my class from the Haas School of Business at the University of California at Berkeley are frequent volunteers.

Nipun has spoken to my classes in New York, London, and San Francisco, and the reaction has been surreal. MBA students who want to be Masters of the Universe and executives who are already on their way become teary-eyed. Give, without expectation, for the sake of giving. They all know there is unspoiled joy in this; they just need to be reminded and shown how.

▣

smile cards bring joy to you as well as others

One of the initiatives started by CharityFocus is Smile Cards. You do an act of anonymous kindness for someone and leave a Smile Card behind. The card explains that some unknown person has performed this service and invites the recipient to "pay it forward" and leave the Smile Card for the next person to do likewise.

To start doing this yourself, go to charityfocus.org, click on "About Us" at the bottom, and then on "Programs." Then click on "Smile Cards" to find out how to get the cards and see hints on how to use them. Get yourself a bunch of cards and start performing your anonymous acts of kindness. By the way, Smile Cards—like most CharityFocus initiatives—are free. The cards you order have already been paid for, and you can choose if and how much you would like to contribute to the effort.

◙

30

Standing on slippery rocks

◘

O K, YOU GET IT. Being other-centered is good for your
well-being. Your mental models, as well as everyone
else's, are ultimately capable of being refuted. And yes, you
intellectually comprehend that we're all—in our own inimi-
table ways—seeking happiness and freedom. But what are the
answers to the questions we raised in the last chapter and never
answered? Do you feel compassion for the person who's trying
to destroy you? How literally do you take the injunction to
turn the other cheek? If you accept that other people's worldviews have the same validity as yours, do you slip into a chaos
where anything is permissible? You're standing on very slip-
pery rocks when you try to reconcile your firmly held notions
of how the world works with those of someone else, especially
when there is a sharp divergence.

One of my MBA students unequivocally laid it on the line
for me. He wasn't being a smart aleck. He was simply intensely

curious and wanted to get to the bottom line as quickly as he could:

===

"Professor Rao, are you telling me there's nothing I have to get, do, or be in order to be happy? That happiness is my very nature and with me always?" he demanded.

"That's correct," I said.

"Then tomorrow, when the alarm rings, I'll hit the snooze button," he said. Then he got warmed up. "Dang the snooze button, I'll throw the clock out the window. From now on, beer and football and TV and girls will figure more prominently in my life. Classes and assignments will figure less, if at all. Why should I do anything at all if all I do is seek happiness and it's with me already?"

He looked at me questioningly. His arms weren't akimbo, but his posture conveyed that impression.

===

The short answer is he was right. You *don't* have to do anything or get anything or be anything to be happy. But you can only get away with what my student suggested *if* you're at a certain level of consciousness. Here's a story to illustrate the point:

===

Sri Ramakrishna was an enlightened sage in nineteenth-century India, and when he left his body, his disciples scattered all over the country. One of them, who later became famous as Swami Brahmananda, was traveling to the holy city of Varanasi when he could walk no more. He hadn't eaten for some days, and it was cold. He lay down under a tree and closed his eyes. He thought that his time had come and was at peace with the idea. The body appears and disappears, dust to dust, and he had long ago come to terms with this as no big deal.

A passing stranger saw the holy man sleeping in the cold and covered him with an expensive shawl. Swami Brahmananda thought, *How wonderful is the universe. I was cold, and it provided a shawl for me.*

Even as he was thinking this, another passerby saw an expensive shawl on an apparently sleeping man and quietly took it away. Swami Brahmananda burst out laughing and thought, *How marvelous is the play of the universe! Even as I was giving thanks for a warm shawl, it disappeared. How perfectly jolly!* He was ecstatic with mirth.

═══

If you are at a similar level of consciousness as the holy man, then you can do nothing and still be happy. But somehow I doubt that any of us are there. With that in mind, I informed my disappointed student, "No, it won't work for you to loll around and do nothing."

Remember that you can only act from the level of consciousness where you are. Don't berate yourself for not having the compassion of the Buddha or Jesus. Don't try to imitate them; it's fruitless. Don't try to mimic their actions either—you won't get the same result.

Instead, do the best you can from where you are. If you're attacked, defend yourself. If you have a vision of how the world should be, try to bring it about. Remember the inspired words of Abraham Lincoln in his second inaugural address:

"With malice toward none, with charity for all, with firmness in the right as God gives us to see the right, let us strive on to finish the work we are in; to bind up the nation's wounds; to care for him who shall have borne the battle, and for his widow and his orphan—to do all which may achieve and cherish a just and lasting peace, among ourselves, and with all nations."

Lincoln acknowledged human frailty and imperfection and did not proclaim that he was "right," but acted according to what "God gives us to see the right." You can't do better than this. Be open to the possibility that what you see as right today may not be so tomorrow.

Consciously consider the impact of whatever you do on all the parties affected and have the intention that your actions will be of benefit to them all. You won't always succeed, but the outcome is more likely to be optimal. Most important, invest in the process, not the outcome. Read Chapter 14 again to refresh your understanding of this concept.

Sometimes, buried in the headlines that proclaim calamities, we forget how far we've come as a species. There is little doubt that the level of consciousness is increasing around the globe, despite pockets that seem to be retrogressing. A bare 150 years ago, it was common for some human beings to own other human beings—a concept that is anathema to most people today. There are organizations like the United Nations to ensure that the needs of the poorest people are met, no matter how ineffectual such organizations seem to be. There is support—at least vocal support—for environmental safeguarding, the abolition of child labor, the banning of land mines, and many similar issues. Granted, there is also hypocritical posturing and not much action in proportion to the talk, but the very fact that these issues are being debated is a huge step forward from a hundred years ago.

Your task is not to be discouraged at what could be done but isn't. It is to do your bit to help raise the level of consciousness even further, and the best and only way you can do this is to work on yourself.

◙

who renounced more? an instructive tale

The following story has deep implications. Reflect on them and be guided by your intuition as you internalize the lessons:

⸝⸝

Reynald was a wealthy businessman who was known for his hedonistic lifestyle. He imbibed freely and maintained a large cellar of the finest vintages. He was fond of women and had a discreet stable of mistresses—at least it was discreet until the tabloids broke the story. Many a former employee leaked tales of his epic rages, all-night sessions in the height of business battles, and his single-minded pursuit of wealth and power. He unashamedly and unabashedly allied himself with those who could help him further his aims and readily discarded them when he no longer needed their help. He was shrewd enough to do so with a smile, because he knew that the wheel always turns and he might well need to call on them again.

Reynald also supported the work of the Master, a sage known for his abstemiousness. The Master mobilized his disciples to build hospitals for the poor, schools for children of illiterate parents, and soup kitchens for the homeless. The Master himself lived simply, partaking of a single meal each day, sleeping on the floor, and spending his time in prayer and contemplation.

"How I admire your renunciation," Reynald exclaimed one day. "How can you give up so many wonderful pleasures to live the way you do?"

"Me? I have given up but a trifle," said the Master with genuine astonishment. "The body exists but for the blink of an eye, and these sensual pleasures fade altogether too soon and leave pain in their wake. You, on the other hand, have renounced eternal, never-ending joy and the deep purpose that gives meaning to all life. You are, by far, the greater renouncer!"

31

What counts
is what's inside you

□

ARE YOU READY to move on? Have you ever felt angry, envious, afraid, exhausted, disgusted, drained, anxious, betrayed, confused, cheated, frustrated, guilty, humiliated, impatient, inadequate, vulnerable, manipulated, embarrassed, neglected, heartbroken, trapped, fatigued, victimized, resentful, or worn out?

Think back over your life and pinpoint the last occasion when you experienced each of these feelings. Was it recently? Are far too many of them your constant companions? Pick one—say, anger. Why do you feel angry? Think about this carefully; it's not a trivial question.

I've heard many responses, some of them cleverly self-serving:

□ I can't bear to see helpless people being taken advantage of.
□ Our politicians are such hypocritical, corrupt animals.

- ▣ My boss/colleague/spouse/friend behaved so unfairly.
- ▣ He tried to cheat me.
- ▣ She lied to me.
- ▣ He didn't do what he said he would.
- ▣ Yet again, she was late for an important meeting.
- ▣ I paid a lot of money for it, and it was defective.
- ▣ I was promised an ocean view, but I had to stand on a stepstool and use binoculars to see the ocean.
- ▣ The loan officer never told me there would be additional costs at closing.
- ▣ She had an affair and concealed it.

And on, and on, and on.

What reason did you come up with? Was it one of these or something similar? Do you really believe this is why you get angry?

There is only one reason for getting angry, and that is because you have anger inside you. True, any of a number of events can trigger it, but the only reason you get angry is because you always lug around a load of anger.

The same is true of all the other emotions listed earlier; you feel them because you carry them around with you. But you're quite willing to ascribe their existence to some external factor that's beyond your control.

Think of a piñata. It is struck repeatedly with sticks, kicked, and broken open. What comes out? Chocolates and sweets and all kinds of goodies. Why is this? Because that's what's in it.

The universe has its own ways of subjecting you to stress and strain, and they are scintillating in their diversity. You never know where the ball that will bean you is coming from. But your reactions are far less diverse—they're the emotions listed in the first paragraph of this chapter. Those emotions are what's in you, so when you're pressed, that's what comes out.

The only way to not experience these negative emotions is to transmute what is within you. The exercises in this book, if done regularly and conscientiously, will start the process. Chapter 32 will be particularly helpful, as it explains how external influences affect your internal state.

There is something else that you think is outside that is really inside. More accurately, it can only flourish inside, but you have to seed and grow and nurture it. This is passion. Countless people have come up to me after one of my public talks to say how much they love the vision I hold out. They want to live a life where they find deep meaning in their work, where they're passionate about what they do and care about the organization and its people. But they confess they don't really feel that way in their current situation.

I ask them to write a description of their ideal job, one that would make them feel the way they want to. They come back with a list of anywhere from ten to thirty parameters. They specify its geographical location, their remuneration, the amount of travel involved, the size of their office, their boss's nature, their colleagues and customers, and much more. They're utterly convinced that if they had a job like that, they would be passionate about it.

Their faces drop when I tell them they're utterly mistaken. That it would be next to impossible to find a position that had all the characteristics they've listed, and even if some miracle produced such a position for them, it wouldn't take long for them to become equally disenchanted in that job.

What they—and most people—don't realize is that passion doesn't exist in the job—it exists in *you*! You can't find it outside; you have to discover it inside. And if you can't ignite it in yourself right where you are now, you're unlikely to find it elsewhere.

But here is the strange part. Once you start kindling that enthusiasm wherever you are, your job mysteriously transforms itself and what you're seeking miraculously arrives. It may or may not be with the same organization, but your ideal job will find you if you do the following exercise conscientiously. You will also benefit greatly if you let these quotes seep into your consciousness:

> *Caring about our work, liking it, even loving it, seems strange when we see work only as a way to make a living. But when we see work as a way to deepen and enrich all of our experience, each one of us can find this caring within our hearts, and awaken it in those around us, using every aspect of our work to learn and grow. . . . Every kind of work can be a pleasure. Even simple household tasks can be an opportunity to exercise and expand our caring, our effectiveness, our responsiveness. As we respond with caring and vision to all work, we develop our capacity to respond fully to all of life. Every action generates positive energy that can be shared with others. These*

qualities of caring and responsiveness are the greatest gift we can offer.

—Tarthang Tulku

What you receive depends on what you give. The workman gives the toil of his arm, his energy, his movement; for this the craft gives him a notion of the resistance of the material and its manner of reaction. The artisan gives the craft his love; and to him the craft responds by making him one with his work. But the craftsman gives the craft his passionate research into the laws of nature which govern it; and the craft teaches him Wisdom.

—René Schwaller de Lubicz

◻

you can transform your job

Think about this: every time you complain about your job, every time you're disheartened because of something that happens at work, you're focusing exclusively on the two or three things that are wrong with it. More accurately, you're focusing on the two or three things that *you think* are wrong with it and completely ignoring the twenty or thirty things that are actually pretty good about it.

Get a notebook and start recording the things that are pretty good about your work and organization. Do you have some colleagues who are decent human beings and with whom you love to spend time? Write that down. Are there some tasks you're responsible for that you really enjoy? Put that down too. When you're actively looking for what is good about your job—including the fact that you have one!—many things that you previously ignored will come to your attention. Record all of these things and celebrate them.

Spend several days to a week doing this. It will have the effect of changing your mind-set from one of dissatisfaction to "Now that I really think about it, things are actually pretty good!" From this emotional space, pick something about your job that you particularly like and is also important to the organization. Devise a project to increase that component in your work life, and give yourself one month in which to accomplish it. Whatever you choose should have a strong learning element—it should push you out of your comfort zone and help you acquire new skills.

For example, are some of your clients absolute gems? Your project could entail acquiring more customers like that. Or it could be moving your relations with more customers to that level. You get to decide.

Every day, do something that helps you accomplish your goal. It's good if you can do it first thing in the morning but not essential. At the end of the month, evaluate your progress. It's OK to give yourself more time if you need it, but be sure that you're scrupulous in taking some action every day that will help you achieve the goal you've set for yourself.

If you do this in a disciplined fashion for a year, you'll complete four to six projects, each of which will have increased some area of your job that turns you on. You'll also find that you're no longer in the job you started out with. You'll be on your way to reaching your ideal job.

Here's something you need to realize: your "ideal job" doesn't exist. It's something that you craft over time, assembling the pieces as if it were a temporal jigsaw puzzle. You don't find it. You wake up one morning and realize you're in it.

◙

32

What to do when fear strikes

◙

THERE IS A new specter that haunts many people in the
workplace today. Quite possibly you have felt it too or
seen it close up or even tangled with it. It is fear—raw, untram-
meled fear. Fear of being without a job, fear of being unable
to maintain your accustomed living standard, fear of downward mobility in all its varied incarnations.

In a capitalist society with relatively free labor markets,
involuntary job loss has always been a possibility and is
accepted as such. But there is also the belief that other jobs
would be available and that this event would be nothing more
than a temporary inconvenience.

This changed in the United States for blue-collar workers
in the 1970s and 1980s. Well-paid union jobs with good benefits disappeared forever by the tens of thousands. Bedrock
industries such as steel and automobile manufacturing started

hurting, and vast swaths of the country went from manufacturing meccas to rust-belt symbols.

The same malaise has now hit white-collar America. Headlines scream about increasing unemployment rates. There are heartrending stories about the long-term unemployed and their emotional and medical problems. Job loss has become the most important reason that homes are foreclosed. A college education used to be a pretty good guarantee of employment. This is no longer true, and the line of the educated unemployed is long and growing longer.

Thus, many in the workplace with jobs have fear in their hearts. This fear is physically constricting and mentally debilitating. It causes people to hold onto jobs that they find nauseating. It prevents them from being authentic and leads to a sharp increase in toxic workplace politics.

═

It was a small item in the financial press, but Tim caught it and his stomach constricted. A private equity outfit had acquired the third largest firm in his industry and "was looking for other acquisitions." Would his company be next? Private equity guys were vultures. They said that they "liberated value" and made the businesses they took over more efficient. What they actually did was strip an acquired company bare, reduce expenditures drastically by laying off lots of workers, load the entity with debt from which they paid themselves a huge fee to recoup their money, and then spin the remainder out in a public offering that gave them even more lucre. The weakened company would either fail or totter along, but they didn't care. He cursed the

financial engineers who played such an important part in the economic scene.

He turned back to his PC. There was an e-mail reminder that he
had to pay his credit card bill. He had set this up so he would never be
late and incur the increasingly horrendous late fees. There was a siz-
able charge from an upscale store. His wife had bought two evening
dresses intending to decide between them at leisure. Unable to make
up her mind she had kept both. Why did she have to be so profligate?
He worked such long hours that she felt this was her due. She just
didn't understand how precarious his standing in the company was.
There was nothing wrong with his performance; he was very highly
compensated and was sure to stand out on any spreadsheet scrutiniz-
ing expenses. Every time he tried to talk to her about this they got into
a screaming fight.

His secretary buzzed. It was time for the staff meeting to discuss
Abigail's proposal. She had an MBA from a top school and was the
ultimate eager beaver—always coming up with proposals to do something or stop doing something or do something differently. The problem was that most of her ideas were half-baked and took no account
of the realities of a resource-constrained company with conservative
upper management. Abigail reported to him, and he had tried to quell
some of her more outlandish ventures. But she had gone over his head
to his boss's boss, who had taken a shine to her "innovative thinking."
He had to call a meeting to discuss each harebrained idea and document why he squelched it. He suspected that Abigail was using her
connection with the senior executive to undercut him.

He was surprised to see his boss, Al, at the meeting. Apparently
Al was free and thought he would see what was going on. Tim felt an

instant of panic and forced it down. Was Al there to build a case for letting him go? He wished he had spent more time reading Abigail's report. Her writing was so long-winded and filled with jargon that he had gotten into the habit of just skimming any memo from her and then filing it. There were only six people at the meeting—many of the department heads were missing, which was not surprising because they had work to do, and he had quietly let them know that Abigail's ideas were not a priority. But it did not look good with Al there.

Tim praised Abigail for her initiative but pointed out that her idea would eat up virtually the entire discretionary budget and require hiring at least two people. He was prepared to do that only if she had evidence that doing so would have a reasonable chance of success. An academic paper touting the strategy and showing spectacular results obtained in an experiment involving students was not enough. "Do I actually have to tell her this?" he fumed silently. He could have been more forthright and gotten rid of her or told her exactly what she had to do if he was surer of himself. He didn't know how well plugged-in she was within the company. He did know that her father was a golfing buddy of two of the board members.

After the meeting he got back to work. Jim, one of his direct reports, had also put together a proposal that called for significant resources—even more than Abigail had asked for. What made it different was that Jim had assembled solid evidence and made a darn good case for his proposal. He had piloted a small experiment using real products with the company's customers, and the results had been outstanding. Normally Tim would have approved Jim's proposal and gone to bat to get additional funding for it, but not now—not when then market was so uncertain, and not with the higher-ups looking so closely at numbers and second-guessing every decision.

Should he preemptively suggest decreasing headcount in his division? That would be a good way to get rid of Abigail, and no one could accuse him of unfairness if he also dropped the axe on Jim. No, not Jim—he was a hard worker and really good at what he did. Perhaps Ralph . . .

═══

Can you empathize with Tim? Have you experienced at least some of what he is going through? I receive reports from the frontlines of major companies every day. People are more reluctant to say what they really feel, more ready to acquiesce to what their bosses want, less willing to take actions that depart from "normal" practice, and more disengaged from the jobs they are striving to retain.

Go back and read Chapter 16 again. You feel fear and insecurity because you create drama in your head. Unconsciously you tell yourself a story—a story about loss, deprivation, and horrible things that could happen—and there is enough power in your telling it that negative feelings reach out and grab you. You entirely forget that what you fear may never come to pass, that it is merely one possible way in which your life can unfold. Even if the eventuality that scares you does come about, it is by no means clear that it is a "bad thing." Mark Twain is reputed to have said that he suffered a great many misfortunes in his life, most of which never happened. That is precisely true of you also.

I remember reading an article written by a journalist who interviewed many extreme athletes, those who find normal athletic achievement rather ordinary and instead push hard to reach far higher peaks. Thus, they may go beyond a marathon to do a sixty-mile run, or do two Ironmans back to back, or not just climb the Matterhorn but attempt its impossible north face in winter.

The journalist noted that there was one thing true of every person he interviewed—they all had an incredible ability to live in the moment. "When your muscles are screaming; when you are so winded that each step is a Herculean effort; when you are cold, tired, and sleepy, you just cannot think of how much more distance you have to cover," one of them said. "If you do think of that, even fleetingly, you are dead. You just have to focus in taking the next step and then the one after that."

This is a very important lesson that you can apply to your life as well. The following exercise shows how.

▣

the next step and only that

The next time you are tormented by fear and uncertainty, pause and take a deep breath. Recognize that you have just embarked on a journey—one that you do not wish to go on and that takes you to a place you do not want to spend time in. What if you lose your job, can't get another for months, can't make your mortgage payments and your house gets foreclosed, your spouse files for divorce, and your kids have to drop out of their Ivy League college and go to a state school instead?

This is a story line, just one of many. Could any of this happen? Sure, but you deal with it when and if it does occur. Pay attention to it only to the extent necessary so you can take prudent preventive action and then dismiss it altogether. Then focus ferociously on what you have to do. If you are hugely productive, you will not be made redundant. And even if you are, you will bounce back fast and higher. This is a skill, and you can learn it. In fact, it is mandatory that you learn it if you are not to be bowled over by the forces of turbulent change that grow stronger each year.

Let me repeat: imagine the worst thing that can happen to you only to determine what you can pragmatically do to forestall it. Then banish it utterly from your mind. Focus insistently, intensely, exclusively on what you can do, and do it with complete dedication. The outcome will be what it is, and you will deal with it if it appears. In doing this, you banish the ghosts that would otherwise prey on you, and you discover that dedicated action brings you its own reward in increased joy.

Few people have had more important things weighing on their minds than General Dwight D. Eisenhower did in the seventy-two hours immediately preceding D-Day. The fate of the free world and the lives of hundreds of thousands of soldiers—and millions of other people— depended on his decisions. But he slept soundly and peacefully. He explained why much later in a candid interview. After consulting with his field commanders, he decided what he would do under each possible weather condition that could arise. Having done that, he simply concentrated on making sure that preparations were complete. He did not agonize over what could happen and the number of ways in which the most ambitious invasion ever undertaken could go awry. He was prepared to deal with each eventuality if it arose. He knew the outcome was beyond his control, so he focused on the process and gave it his very best.

You can do likewise. You *should* do likewise.

33

Beware the stories you tell and the company you keep!

▣

Y OU SPEND MUCH of your time telling stories to yourself about yourself. You don't realize it, but you do. You also don't comprehend the extent to which you experience the world as you do because of the nature of the stories you tell yourself.

Here, for example, is a tale I frequently hear: "My job is OK. Not great, but tolerable. The company is fine, the pay is on the low side but not impossibly so, and the people are generally nice. My boss is a problem. He simply doesn't appreciate what I do and is a micromanager. I'm trying hard to build a relationship with him, but it's hard because I don't respect him at all. I don't think he'll recommend me for the promotion that I should have gotten last year. I wish I could find some way to get him to really like me."

What's not immediately clear is that there are several story lines in this short lamentation. First there's the story that being in a great job depends on outside stuff like company, pay, and so forth. Then there's the story that the boss is important and has to be placated somehow because he bestows promotions, raises, and similar plums. Then there's the story that active effort has to be extended not in doing the job—though this may be taken as a given—but in trying to build a relationship with this powerful creature called "boss."

Can you recognize the story lines in the tales you tell about your situation?

The important lesson is that none of these stories are absolutely true. You—yes, you—can decide to change them. When you do, you'll discover the new story you tell is just as valid as the old one and bears up to scrutiny equally well.

I encourage people in my programs to embrace the story that the boss doesn't and can't "give" goodies like raises, promotions, plum assignments, and the like. These come from the universe, and your boss can neither originate nor stop them. He is merely the instrument of delivery. Think of your boss as the FedEx guy who gives you a package. You say, "Thank you," because you're polite, but you don't think the package came from him. He was merely the instrument of delivery, and someone else sent the package.

Think of your boss in exactly the same way—he's a FedEx guy. You'll be polite and professional. You'll heed him in the organizational role he occupies and try to maintain an amicable working relationship. But you won't go into a tizzy in an attempt to propitiate him. Numerous people have found this to be a liberating take on what was previously an unpleasant situation.

Here is another illustration of how the stories you tell affect you:

===

Nancy was attractive, well groomed, and highly intelligent. She also carried scars from terrible childhood experiences. A broken home, abuse by her father (or stepfather, neither she nor her mother was sure), hard drugs, foster care, juvenile detention, and much more. Being bright, she graduated from college and then from a prestigious professional school, but then she ran into a brick wall. Companies would hire her because of her education and obvious smarts, then they would discover that she lacked social skills, was angry and combative, and couldn't accept rules and authority, so they would fire her. Eventually, as the string of short-term stints on her résumé grew, organizations stopped offering her jobs altogether.

The story Nancy used to tell herself was, "I'm the way I am because of the horrible things that happened to me as a child. There's nothing I can do about this. I have no money for therapy, and anyway, that would take years."

With some coaching and encouragement, she began telling herself a different story: "I've had a set of experiences that most people can't even imagine. Because of this, I can empathize with people at a much deeper level. What others call adversity doesn't affect me because I've known far worse."

It took a few months of repeating this to herself, but the story took root. She started relating better to people and got her temper and aggression under better control. One of her former bosses decided to give her a second chance, and Nancy began to turn her life around.

===

Become acutely aware of the stories you believe. Recognize that you believe them not because they're "true" but because they're what you tell yourself. Change these stories, and your life changes.

There's another way in which you can start transforming your life, and this method is even more powerful if you use it in conjunction with whatever new story you start telling yourself. Start hanging out with people who are already where you want to be. As Warren Buffett said, "It's better to hang out with people better than you. Pick out associates whose behavior is better than yours, and you'll drift in that direction."

The *sangha*, or community of monks, is one of the pillars of Buddhism. The Buddha himself established such a community as an aid to those on the path of awakening and as a means of preserving his teaching in pure form. Today, the term is used more loosely, and there are also sanghas of laypeople who support each other.

The concept of a fraternity of like-minded individuals helping each other is both appealing and effective and has been propagated by many, including steel magnate Andrew Carnegie and his protégé Napoleon Hill, of *Think and Grow Rich* fame. Peer group influence is very strong, and much work has been done in this area of psychology. Unquestionably, over time, you tend to absorb and inculcate the values of your peers. This is true of gang members, soldiers in close-knit fighting units, and monks in monasteries.

Sociologists are just beginning to recognize what a powerful principle this is. A recent article in the *New York Times Magazine* reports that social scientists Nicholas Christakis and

James Fowler found some solid evidence that ". . . good behaviors—like quitting smoking or staying slender or being happy—pass from friend to friend as if they were contagious viruses. . . . And the same was true of bad behaviors—clusters of friends appeared to 'infect' each other with obesity, unhappiness and smoking. Staying healthy isn't just a matter of your genes and your diet, it seems. Good health is also a product, in part, of your sheer proximity to other healthy people."

It's not so easy, however, to deliberately make use of this principle. If you want to be a strong chess player, you want to hang out with grand masters. The problem is that grand masters won't want to hang out with you. It generally doesn't work for you to decide, "This is the kind of person I want to spend time with." You have to make some progress toward *becoming* that sort of person yourself before others will first tolerate and then welcome your company.

▣

the company you keep decides where you go and how you feel

Make a list of all your friends and the professional colleagues with whom you spend discretionary time. Taking one at a time, go over the interactions you have had with them. Recognize that everyone has good days and bad days and make allowances for that, but see how you feel on average after spending time in their company. Are you energized, optimistic, upbeat, enthusiastic, and looking forward to the morrow? Or are you dejected, pessimistic, and full of dark, moody feelings? Does each person pull you on an upward path or send you into a downward spiral?

If it's the latter, consciously notice when you start on the downward trajectory and make an attempt to change direction. If your friend consistently won't let this happen, it may not be a bad idea to ease back from your relationship and eventually abandon it.

Now observe yourself. What kind of comments do you make? Do you complain a lot? Do you make sardonic remarks that are funny but make others wrong? Do you commiserate with people who have suffered misfortune and push them deeper into a negative space, or do you grab hold of them and show them that the sun is shining and, somewhere, there are rainbows?

Make it a point to always bring up the spirits of whomever you're around. You'll discover that when you're firmly anchored in this habit, your own inner life is greatly enriched and people want to be with you.

Remember you can't decide to bring "good company" into your life. You have to attract it. This exercise will help you do that.

▣

34

A new model of the world

FOR DECADES, MY professional life has focused on teaching "Creativity and Personal Mastery" (CPM). Despite its popularity and proven ability to transform people's lives, most find it difficult to say what it is. This is true even of people who have taken classes and attended my workshops.

So what exactly is CPM? This is highly relevant to you, because this book—like my program—is designed to help you view the universe in a totally fresh way. If you conscientiously do the exercises in this book, they will cumulatively change the way you look at the world, and as this new worldview becomes embedded in your psyche, you literally become a different person.

Let me spell out the worldview I'm encouraging you to adopt:

▣ You *can* live a joyful, intensely fulfilling life. In fact, you should resolutely settle for nothing less. You have only one life—not a "personal" life and a "professional" life—and this should be hugely exhilarating. Even tackling challenges should be fun.

◉ Your mental chatter is the prime culprit in leading you astray. Once you recognize this, you can direct that chatter and make it your friend in your quest for your ideal job and life.

◉ Your mental models can also blindside you. The problem is not that you have mental models, it's that you don't *recognize* that you have mental models. Every time you're stuck in some persistent, distasteful situation, you are using one or more mental models that are not serving you well.

◉ You can't live a thoroughly fulfilling life if you live in a me-centered world. That's just the way it is. If you want to experience joy, you have to devote your energies to a cause that's bigger than you are. A cause that brings a greater good to a greater community. You have a lot of flexibility in defining both "greater good" and "greater community."

◉ A terrific way to start is by having a default emotional attitude of appreciation and gratitude. This can be cultivated and is far superior to being a whining complainer. Don't be a carping, griping, morose, disgruntled individual perpetually dejected because the universe will not conform to your rigid expectations.

◉ You live in a benevolent universe, one that wants to help you and gives you everything you need at precisely the time you need it. You just have to recognize this, acknowledge it, and celebrate it.

▣ Miracles happen regularly, and you can create them. You can't create—at least not all the time—a specific miracle at a specific time. You *can* create a life where unexpected good fortune—miracles!—is a regular occurrence. Trust me, this is far better than living in a universe where coincidences happen occasionally.

▣ The world you think you live in is a construct. It's not *the* reality; it's *a* reality. You can deconstruct parts of it that aren't working and construct an "alternative" reality. You will do this many times in many different areas of your life.

▣ By all means, work toward a goal, but stop fretting about outcomes. They're beyond your control anyway. Invest in the process, not the outcome. Accept the outcome, whatever it is, as joyfully as you can. This becomes a new starting point for you.

▣ You are *always* playing a role, whether or not you recognize it. Shakespeare had it right: "All the world's a stage." Play your role with gusto. Don't relate to people based on the role they're playing—boss, banker, administrative assistant, and so on—but as one human being to another. We're all in this predicament called life together, and none of us has a clue what's going on, so stop giving yourself airs.

▣ Laughter trumps everything. Read one P. G. Wodehouse novel a week, and you'll be amazed at how red the roses are and what a nice fragrance comes from sewers. (OK, I stuck that one in there for laughs, but there's more than an element of truth in it!)

▣ It's your job to be of service—this is a corollary to avoiding a me-centered existence. Help others for the sake of doing so, not to plant an obligation or bask in thanks.

▣ Don't ever, ever, *ever* hand over the keys of your well-being and happiness to *anyone*. You don't have to.

▣ You will run into many "problems" that you simply won't be able to solve. You'll have to grow out of them and become bigger than the problems.

▣ Mindfulness is your vehicle for retaining your stability when you are hit by tidal waves. Be aware that you're the actor, not the character.

If you successfully embrace all of these elements, you'll go deeper into the rabbit hole and discover that you have actually found a path that takes you to a vast, uncharted territory where your personal quest ends; here you discover that there's nowhere to go, nothing to do, and no one to do it. Discovering this simple truth may well take several lifetimes.

▣

a powerful tool: become the witness

The next time you're angry, frightened, jealous, or in the grip of any strong negative emotion, imagine that you're an invisible entity suspended a foot above your head. From this vantage point, simply observe yourself. You are simply a recorder, not a judge. Don't evaluate your actions and label them "good" or "bad." Simply observe them.

You may observe that "she said she would wash the dishes immediately but is watching 'Desperate Housewives' instead. She's feeling guilty and somewhat uneasy, because she knows she's violating a pact she made with herself; this is preventing her from truly enjoying the show. In the back of her mind, she's aware that she'll be so sleepy when the program finishes that she'll go straight to bed and wake up to a sink full of dirty dishes. Cleaning them will make her late for work and set her whole day back. . . ."

I repeat—don't evaluate, just observe dispassionately. If you can sink into the role of witness, you'll find that your strong emotions no longer have the power to sway you as they once did, and lasting behavior change happens with little conscious effort on your part.

▢

35

Where does your journey take you?

□

Life is a journey. You come alone; you depart alone; and in between you have companions, some of whom are with you for a short time, some for a long time, and some who keep flitting in and out at various intervals. What you have probably not considered until now is that, within this grand journey, you make many side trips, and each of these is a journey by itself.

Have you spent an hour reading this book and thinking of its application to your life? That is a journey. So is going to work. So is having an argument with your spouse, criticizing your teenage daughter, and serving as a volunteer firefighter.

Do you watch prime-time TV? That is also a journey, one that takes you to a place where bored forty-something housewives have affairs with twenty-something gardeners while their husbands are fooling around with glamorous assistants. Or to a place where terrible things are happening to the country, it's about to be destroyed in a nuclear holocaust, and only one man can save it—by tying the bad guy to the steering wheel of a car and breaking all his fingers until he gives up the name of the next bad guy and on and on until the final bad guy is thwarted. Of course, the ultimate baddie escapes to reappear next season.

Does this strike a chord in you? Do you listen to the news on the radio—the rapes, fires, murders, and shootings that play on in endless loops? Do you see that the *only* thing you do in life is go on journeys, big and small?

There's nothing wrong with any of this, but the next time you're about to embark on one of these journeys, pause for a moment and ask yourself these questions: Where is this journey taking me, and is it a place where I want to spend time? Is it a place that makes me happy to be alive, that brings out the best in me and inspires me in some way? Or is it a place that brings out hidden fears and insecurities and makes me more of a clinging, dissatisfied clod who whines about how the universe refuses to adapt to my whims? Or is it somewhere in between?

If you ask yourself these questions many times each day and answer them honestly until it becomes a regular habit, you'll notice that subtle but significant changes start taking place in your life. You'll stop taking many journeys that you presently take unthinkingly. You'll notice changes in the types of books you read, the movies you see, the TV shows you watch, the friends you associate with, the topics of conversation you bring up, the amount and kinds of products you buy, the politicians you vote for, the charities you contribute to, the food you eat, and the length of time you shower.

The changes will be gradual at first, but many small ones will eventually merge to produce some pretty drastic rearrangement of the fabric of your life. If you have done the exercises in this book conscientiously and hold firm to the intent of living a completely fulfilled, utterly joyous life, then this constant questioning will guide you to the path you need to take. One day, you'll realize you're leading the life you dreamt about today. It may or may not be the one you currently visualize in terms of what you have, but it will be better than you can imagine in terms of who you are.

◫

let it go

Sit back, take a deep breath, and really think about what I'm about to share with you. Don't simply understand it intellectually. Let it sink into your gut so you have a visceral communion with it.

Would you agree that, if a cosmic laser beam magically appeared and vaporized a single random grain of sand from one of the beaches on Earth, it would be no big deal? I'll take your assent for granted. (I haven't had anyone argue with me about this yet.)

Now imagine that our sun—good ol' Sol—were to go supernova. It would expand instantly until it engulfed Mercury, Venus, Earth, Mars, and most of the asteroid belt. All of the problems you're concerned about—your insecure job and inadequate salary, the impending and unwelcome visit of your in-laws, crime and religious fundamentalism, global warming—they'd all disappear instantly. Poof! Gone! Along with you and your ego and your other paltry botherations.

There are more than 100 billion stars like our sun—which is quite an unremarkable galactic citizen—in our galaxy. From maps of the universe plotted with the help of the Hubble Space Telescope, we know there are upward of 200 billion galaxies, and each of these has an average of 100 billion stars. And we know that these cumulatively represent a tiny fraction of the mass of the universe—there's more out there than we can fathom.

So on a cosmic scale, if our entire solar system vanished, it would be of considerably less importance than a single grain of sand disappearing from one of our beaches.

Think of the unbelievably vast scale of the cosmos and you'll gain a better perspective of the vexations that trouble you. This is the thousand-foot view of your particular situation, and you can cultivate it.

Be happy now. Know that whatever is aggravating you is trivial.

Let it go.

Index

About the Author

□

SRIKUMAR S. RAO conceived "Creativity and Personal Mastery," the pioneering course that was among the most popular and highest rated of any classes at many of the world's top business schools. It remains the only such course to have its own alumni association. His work has been covered by major media, including the *New York Times*, the *Wall Street Journal*, the *Financial Times*, *Time*, *Fortune*, *BusinessWeek*, the *London Times*, the *Guardian*, and the *Daily Telegraph*. CNN, PBS, Voice of America, and dozens of other television and radio stations have interviewed him.

Please visit srikumarsrao.com for many tools and useful resources. You can follow him on Twitter at @srikumarsrao.